Planting
The Impatience

The Gift of Transformative
Metaphor in Three Easy Steps

Planting
The Impatience

The Gift of Transformative
Metaphor in Three Easy Steps

Dr. K. U. Brügge

BOOKS

Winchester, UK
Washington, USA

First published by O-Books, 2011
O-Books is an imprint of John Hunt Publishing Ltd., Laurel House, Station Approach,
Alresford, Hants, SO24 9JH, UK
office1@o-books.net
www.o-books.com

For distributor details and how to order please visit the 'Ordering' section on our website.

Text copyright: K. U. Brügge 2010

ISBN: 978 1 84694 713 1

A CIP catalogue record for this book is available from the British Library.

Design: Stuart Davies

Printed in the UK by CPI Antony Rowe
Printed in the USA by Offset Paperback Mfrs, Inc

We operate a distinctive and ethical publishing philosophy in all
areas of our business, from our global network of authors to
production and worldwide distribution.

CONTENTS

List of Tables

For Louise and Leah

Stood there boldly
Sweatin' in the sun
Felt like a million
Felt like number one
The height of summer
I'd never felt that strong
Like a rock
Bob Seger, Like a Rock

Preface

Many years ago I sat in a coaching session with an executive of a major retail chain. This particular person, besides having many responsibilities, had difficulty just switching off. He suffered from chronic restlessness and was highly driven. He simply could not sit down and let the world pass him by. He had become blasé about his many overseas trips, including hundreds of business trips to New York City alone. Work and his hectic schedule seemed to engulf him completely. He didn't have his diary, it had him. He did little for himself by way of enjoyment; his two luxury cars stood in their garages as 'investments'. He told me that he envied and romanticized people doing 'ordinary things' like queuing at the movies. To others, his life was extraordinary; to him, theirs was. He said that he wished he could switch places. The thrill was gone.

After some coaching sessions and during a follow-up (this was before I had started to develop the metaphor animation method), this executive said to me: *'This weekend I will plant the impatiens'* (a flower). Although meant literally, the metaphorical meaning of this comment struck me like a bolt out of the blue. Here was a man that was terminally impatient, intending to 'plant the impatiens'! I don't think his comment was just arbitrary, but rather a reflection of an unconscious change process embodied by the flower as a symbol. By that time he had already implemented many of the life changes we had talked about, including sitting on his balcony in his dressing gown for a whole day, overlooking the Indian Ocean. He had also taken his precious sports car for a long drive along a coastal road; top down, wind blowing his hair back, without worrying about putting mileage on it.

What struck me was the generative and positive nature of the metaphor and that it emerged as all the change was happening.

I thought to myself: if a generative metaphor arises so spontaneously, perhaps it will work the *other way round*, i.e. to generate a metaphor *up-front* as a facilitation catalyst and frame for change. I subsequently verified this with other clients, noticing that the metaphors they were using changed (from negative to positive) as they themselves were changing. Metaphors, it turns out, are both change instruments and markers of change.

I am eternally thankful as a vessel to receive the above.

May the book bring you the change that you want.

K.U. Brügge, Mount Grace, 17 March 2010
www.drkaybrugge.com

Acknowledgments

The work by the late David Grove (the originator of 'clean language' who used metaphor therapeutically), Jerome E. Feldman (*From Molecule to Metaphor*), Richard Bandler and John Grinder, James Lawley and Penny Tompkins and others, is hereby acknowledged and has contributed to stimulating my thoughts. The book by the latter two authors in particular has been inspiring. Some of their therapeutic techniques were drawn on and adapted for purposes of positive psychology, a discipline which this book promotes.

Throughout, the words of Bob Seger's 'Like a Rock', laden with metaphor, kept echoing in my mind, pulling me forward, confirming that what I was busy with was true.

A word of thanks to my dear friend Jacques, who told me: 'Aim for the stars; if you strike the treetops you will still be doing OK.'

I would also like to express my appreciation to David Kyslinger for the excellent graphics that he generated, based on my rough sketches.

To my life partner Louise, thank you for assisting with the editing and for your loving support and to my daughter Leah: catch the thermals and soar.

Last but not least, to Carl G. Jung: sadly you passed on before I was born. I so wish that I could have met you to ask you some burning questions and test some ideas. I hope that the methodology set-out in this book in a small way promotes your thoughts and the progression toward a method aimed at change and transformation.

Chapter 1

Introduction

...the unconscious knows more than consciousness does; but it is knowledge of a special sort, knowledge in eternity.
Carl G. Jung, Memories, Dreams, Reflections

How This Book Adds Value

This book is based on a simple suggestion, namely that by eliciting metaphors we bring to life a coherent change model of our subjective/inner life world. By engaging with, and animating[1] our metaphors, thus enhancing or altering how they are put together and organized (bringing the model to life), we change our experiences (whether current or future). Existing conscious associations that no longer work for us are loosened and replaced by new associations that emerge from our unconscious minds. However, metaphor animation allows us to do so without having to enter into the murky domain of logic and reason. Metaphors are positioned at a higher and more abstract level within our minds and therefore provide a sort of mental scaffold on which our thoughts can rest. Our thoughts can only go as high as the scaffold permits. Metaphor animation raises the scaffold, and then pulls it away from underneath you so that you may soar.

The beauty and fruitfulness of engaging with metaphors rather than our ordinary thoughts as expressed in day-to-day language is based on the fact that our reality (and to a large extent our own thoughts) remains *fundamentally unknowable*. Richly textured, metaphors (notably those stated positively) are therefore one of our best shots at fostering understanding and change at a level much deeper and profound than thoughts themselves would permit. Generative and transformative metaphor (reflecting a reality scenario as if it already were real) enriches *how* and *what* we know. As *how* and *what* we know rises to ever higher and more profound levels (through engagement with metaphor), so does personal insight, change and transformation.

Another way of looking at metaphor and the benefit of animating it and its constituent symbols is to think of computer software. If you use word processing software you may be aware that the so-called 'back-end' consists of computer code. It is called the 'back-end' (or program) precisely because it remains hidden from the user. The 'front-end' consists of the neat dashboard, which enables the user to do various things like word processing, including highlighting text, creating headers, etc. The back-end or code constrains what can be done on the dashboard. As those of you who use trial versions of software would know, a portion of the software remains non-functional, until a license is purchased. No amount of clicking will bring the locked and unresponsive features to life. It will be similarly futile to write a message in, say, MS Word, 'asking' the software to unlock the features or even attempt to alter some of the digital gibberish of zeros and ones that drive the whole program. You need to simply buy a license, and – *voilà* – the whole front-end comes to life and is fully functional. Metaphor is much like the back-end of computer software. It drives the dashboard or user interface and sets its capabilities and limitations, which we experience as our ordinary thoughts. The structure and organization of the back-end which would reveal why and how it functions the way it does, usually remains well hidden, i.e. we are not conscious of it. This is also due to the fact that metaphor is more abstract than that which it seeks to comment on/clarify. For example, when we say to someone, 'You are so bright, you have a mind *like* a small planet' something about a 'small planet' is akin to the person's intelligence/mind, e.g. that it is rich and diverse. It certainly is more descriptive than the word 'bright' and stimulates the imagination and meaning-making propensities of our unconscious mind.

We have to be exceptionally self-aware to start identifying the programs (back-end of zeros and ones) that 'drive' our ordinary thoughts and sense of Self. If we were to use our thought processes such as reason and insight to change the back-end, we would soon realize that this is like using the dashboard toolbars to change the program. This is why there are warnings on modern electronic equipment – 'no user serviceable parts inside'. By using rational thoughts to access and influence the back-end (or 'meta-programs'[2]), we are in essence trying to use our thoughts to change our thoughts or even create new and more insightful ones, when it may in fact be the questions we are asking that are leading us astray. These attempts, whilst perhaps yielding modest results at times will always be limited and amount to 'tweaking' of our headspace. This is because we are trying to trade in a psychological currency which is foreign to the back-end and to which it will therefore not respond. We need to go through the mental *'bureau de change'* and exchange our currency into something that will allow for 'trading' between the front-end (ego) and the back-end (unconscious/ Self).

Animating metaphors is one such exchange bureau – it allows us to enter into the somewhat mysterious domain of symbols, which if engaged with, will reveal their basic function and purpose. 'Symbol' comes from the Greek *synbolon*: *syn-* means 'throw' and *-bolon* 'together'. It consists of a signifier and something being signified.[3] These are the tacit or unknown aspects (hidden objects) of the symbol that the animation process set out in this book seeks to tease out, thereby leading to personal change.

Engaging with these symbols will finally reveal an enriched model of the structure of our experiences and allow us to change this structure. If we are lucky it will enable us to bring about quite fundamental personal trans*phor*mation[4] within the metaphor envelope. I have defined the latter as the sealed/contained workspace in which the animation process takes place. In so doing, we reap the fruits of a transformed metaphoric envelope, which brings about a change in how we are fundamentally. Metaphor animation is about going full circle and really recognizing the mental space we started at, for the first time. This is simply because as we change our metaphor, we change too. Thereby we see the same 'reality' in a fundamentally different way. This is true empowerment.

'Stay Within the Lines, Leah'

The seminal idea for this book came in the early 2000s, when my daughter was still at playschool. One day she came home with a sheet of paper that contained outlines of objects, which she had colored-in in her enthusiastic but rather messy fashion, frequently running across the outlines. Underneath it, her teacher had written in red ink, *'Leah, stay within the lines.'* The metaphoric meaning and implications immediately struck me. The lines that make up a frame is what keeps us boxed in, and the frame becomes the theater of our own lives. How these lines are drawn is self-imposed or an acceptance of the frame drawn by others. This notion has been depicted well by the forerunner of reality TV, namely the film *"The Truman Show"*. The producer in the show is really our own (mostly unconscious) thought patterns – the frame which 'directs' us to live our lives in a certain way. Going 'stage exit left' or 'stage exit right', becomes less and less of an option the longer we 'stay within the lines'. It is safe, but also holds us captive. Yet, the curiosity of what lies beyond always prevails.

Other insights struck me at about the same time, namely that metaphors provide a highly enlightening 'frame'. This frame is able to convey our thoughts and feelings to ourselves or others so succinctly yet definitively that it puts long-winded narrative to shame. Positive metaphor can provide us with a highly liberating frame and all the resources we need to make changes in a manner that by far exceeds the capabilities of rational problem solving. By 'staying within the lines' of this frame we are actually able to benefit, unlike the usual mental frames that keep us hemmed in. Working within this frame – called the metaphor envelope – we are able to bring the benefit to bear on our real lives, thereby transcending the 'lines' that keep us constrained there. Negative metaphor (or rather negatively stated metaphor, as metaphor is never 'negative') on the other hand can provide a very rich picture of what is going on inside and what we want to move away from. This also informs the process of animating what I termed the 'RGT' (Remedial, Generative or Transformative) Metaphor.

Another impetus came from my coaching sessions with people from all walks of life. One of the notions that I must have heard the most when people were referring to their life challenges or a desire was that of 'work-life balance'. Personally I am not a fan of this way of trying to make sense or meaning. That which we seek so hard to 'balance' probably does not exist beyond our own thought patterns, and the things we try to balance don't fit into the same category of experience, i.e. that there is a fruitless pursuit in balancing incomparable categories. Let me explain: what is required is not balancing of our work and life per se, but our *attitudes toward it*. At the end of the day, we attend only to our thoughts about 'work' and 'life'. These thoughts, in turn, are driven by very different values, beliefs and expectations (often those of others). If we spend too much time at work, this may be because of fear that we may not be able to 'pay the bills', the need to achieve; the pursuit of wealth, status or power; or passion for what we do. 'Life', on the other hand may be about quality and process – spending time with our spouses and parenting our children – watching the grass grow. Comparatively, the one may look less spectacular than the other. Hence, trying to balance these very differently informed categories of existence did not appear to me convincing, as the 'measurements' we apply to determine if we are achieving 'balance' seemed elusive. It appeared that even when my clients attempted to spend as much time 'doing' life as they did work (which should create the desired balance), they were still not contented. Or, when they poured more energy into 'life', they were 'at work' in their 'mind's eye'; and when they tried to put more energy into 'work', they were mentally 'at home'. Hence, the comparison of 'fruits and vegetables' popped back into my mind as being at the root of 'balance' not achieving desired results. Balancing two different things like 'fruits' and 'vegetables' or 'work' and 'life' seemed unachievable, at least at the level of the ego, which may be more adapt at valuing and validating quantity or measurable experiences. Therefore, I was convinced that my clients' *approach* to work-life balance (which is informed by expectations, 'personality type', values and beliefs, etc.) created the problem. It reinforced my sense that such balancing or the lack thereof only exists within the meaning-making limitations of one's conscious thoughts. An old quote came to mind that talks about the fact that nothing is good or bad. Our thoughts about it give rise to distinctions, which subsequently result in a certain emotional response (mind and body being connected), e.g. feeling stressed; angry; sad; frustrated or happy.

Whilst traveling from the coast to the interior in the land of my birth, Namibia, thousands of corn crickets suddenly appeared next to and on the asphalt. On closer inspection it became evident that those that had ventured onto the road and been killed by cars were subsequently retrieved and devoured by their cannibalistic kin. As can be expected, those that did the retrieving in turn got killed by cars, just to be retrieved and eaten by others. This seemed to create a macabre vicious runaway (no pun intended) cycle, seemingly without resolution. This event left a deep and lasting impression on me and made me think more cyclically about the issue of work-life balance and other life issues presenting themselves to us in a polarized manner. It also made me grasp the role of emotions and shadow emotions (those emotions that spontaneously seem to pop up behind other emotions and influence them) that are part and parcel of the cyclical progression of events.

But – back to the crickets. If we pretend for a moment that the crickets are 'conscious' in a way that we are (can we know for sure that they are not?), and are able to foresee the consequences of their actions, they may face a typical cyclical dilemma. In both instances: (1) the course of action seems not to yield a desirable outcome; and (2) the outcomes seem to create a yearning for the other scenario (thin arrows in the figures below), even though this will also turn out to be non-fulfilling. The risk of getting killed and the emotion of fear seem to create a yearning for the option of not walking onto the road (safe but hungry). *Not* walking into the road and the fear of going hungry seems to create a desire for walking into the road and eating but running the risk of getting killed (see thin arrows). In both instances the emotions are undesirable and the oppositional dilemma created by the 'do' and 'don't' seems hard if not impos-

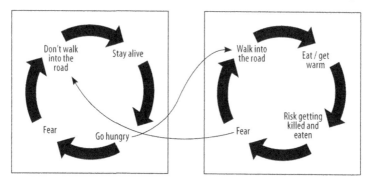

Figure 1.1: The oppositional dilemma faced by Namibian corn crickets

sible to resolve. This is where the resource symbols come in. They tend to offer a resolution(s) which entirely transcends the problem at hand, and which the conscious mind and ego can't seem to overcome.

Something I never got a proper answer to is, 'Why did the corn cricket cross the road?' The jokers among us might say, 'To get to the other side' (another way to make meaning). This funny response is entirely plausible, resulting in the first crickets getting killed, thus setting off the vicious cycles. Other explanations may be that the crickets go onto the road to absorb the warmth radiating from the asphalt. Alternatively, a cricket may have stumbled onto the road by accident, got killed and thus set off the cascade. At the end it doesn't really matter what the first event was. What matters is why it is continuing and most importantly what happens next to arrive at a win-win solution.

Similarly, we would not fully understand events that set off vicious cycles in our own lives. All we have is the memories or experiences of the event. These memories are malleable and with that, the associated emotions. The events, however, have transpired never to return in that exact fashion. Animating metaphors enables us to alter the manner in which we relate to these memories, arresting potentially negative progressions of events and carving a new road.

During about the same time I started re-engaging with the works of Carl Jung. This time around, however, there was a sweetener which came in the form of a casual remark by a colleague about Sandplay Therapy. I became aware of a link between Sandplay Therapy and Carl Jung, who had apparently built a miniature village on the shores of Lake Zürich, during the time when he broke with his mentor, Sigmund Freud. This he had apparently experienced as profoundly distressing. Making manifest his thoughts and feelings by engaging with the sand and building materials of all kinds, he found that it ordered his inner being, brought relief and facilitated his developing a formidable and novel theory. Sandplay Therapy was originated by Dora M. Kalff (a student of Jung's). Something that interested me specifically is the notion of symbols as transformative forces that Jung referred to and which are central to Sandplay's therapeutic outcomes. I believe that mechanisms similar to those prevalent during Sandplay processes may manifest when animating symbols generatively within a metaphor envelope. The symbols may correspond with figurines used in Sandplay; the metaphor envelope with the sand-tray. (The reader is referred to the works of Weinrib and Turner which appear in the reference list of this book.)

Other mechanisms which I believe to be at work during metaphor animation (fully explained later) may include those explored by psychiatrist and neuroscientist Jeffrey M. Schwartz (2005) and others. They have certainly 'cracked the frame' of conventional approaches by suggesting that the manner in which we attend to our experiences alters the brain mechanisms used. In short, active (attentional) engagement with the contents of our thoughts about our experiences will alter not only the latter, but also our brains. This is referred to as 'self-directed neuroplasticity'[5] (p.1310). In other words, the way in which we think acts on our brains much like clay can be molded under the kneading pressure of our hands. Put differently, consciously focusing on our thoughts and then 'reworking' them using language (as metaphor animation does) is seen to be *a causal mechanism* that intervenes in our neural circuitry, including those underlying our emotions. (Mental force acts as a physical force on the brain). The origin of these mechanisms may be 'untraceable in principle' according to Schwartz et al., which may mean – and this requires some blue sky thinking – that the *cause may not be in the brain.* (Did he perhaps include the collective unconscious as a possibility?). The mechanisms that Schwartz refers to are generally applied for purposes of remedying or redirecting neural circuitry associated with a variety of pathological mental states, including Obsessive Compulsive Disorder (OCD).

However, the prospect of directed mindful thoughts (volition) altering both our experiences and our brain circuitry, resulting in emotional self-regulation and growth remains intriguing as an explanation for what happens when we engage with our life world through the 'lens' of animated/animating metaphor. Engaging with transformative metaphor offers a directed attentional window or 'lens', through which to observe, engage with and direct our thoughts and unconscious energy in a manner which is lasting. If this also happens to change our neural circuitry and make it more functional, this can be seen as a bonus. In summary: we first re-focus *outward* onto the RGT metaphor (and away from the negative metaphor), and thereby also re-focus attention *inward* onto the new neural circuits which are formed in accord with the RGT metaphor being animated (a conscious, willed action). First we shape, and then we are shaped.

A Few Simple Guidelines

i. When you engage in the *Metaphor Animation for Personal Transformation (M.A.P.T.)* process, stay within the metaphor envelope or envelope of envelopes[6] at all times. Try to phrase your thoughts within this existing 'virtual reality', which is the metaphor, using the symbols present as your tools or point of reference. You will experience this to be effortless and fun, fueling your curiosity as the process is principally driven by the unconscious mind.

ii. Stay away from logic and reason – different rules and dynamics apply within the envelope that supersedes the ego with its limited perspective. The ego[7] is prone to interpretation and making sense logically. However, the symbols which appear to you don't require interpretation. If the animation process is successful, the breakthroughs or insight you require for change happen quite automatically. This is because the world of symbols is driven by the unconscious[8] mind – the ego is merely the 'gopher' at its service, which finally becomes a humble servant. It creates an environment conducive for the symbols to emerge – it sets the table, like a butler. In order to do so however, it has to relinquish its sense of omnipotence and defer to the Self (the 'whole' you, including the part that you aren't conscious of). The Self, according to Jung, is the organizing force of the psyche – its center and periphery.

iii. When you start experiencing obstacles, intensify your symbol animation process and further insights and options will avail themselves. If you start experiencing seemingly irreconcilable opposites within yourself or issues before you, and the significant tension it creates, it is likely that you are on the brink of transformation. The energy may be uncomfortable, but it is necessary to imbue the metaphor envelope with the stuff required for the animation process to foster the desired breakthrough and renewal. (Not using this energy will soon result in stress and tension and the need to direct it into the environment, whereas applying it in the metaphor domain will put it to constructive use).

iv. Lastly, but probably most importantly: your firm belief that metaphors offer a way *out* of a problem or dilemma and illuminate a way forward which your rational or conscious mind is unable to resolve, is critical to unlock the marvel of transformation through metaphor animation and the power of symbols.

What You Can Expect

By applying the metaphor animation process (see Figure below) described in this book, you can expect to attain:

- remedial changes, which are about problem solving and changing your internal emotional climate; and/or
- generative changes, which are about generating new options and asking different questions about the same issue, thereby altering them or eliminating them (as Bob Seger's song goes, 'The answer's in the question'); and/or
- transformative changes. Transformation involves resolving something by including the original problem (such as an oppositional dilemma) as building blocks, but superseding it in such a manner that the polarity is no longer evident. An analogy would be two pottery vases [which reflect opposites, e.g. internal conflict ('want/don't want'); or having to choose between two equally desirable or undesirable alternatives]. What you could do is take a hammer to both vases and smash them, and use the pieces to build a mosaic table. The table then forms a synthesis of the two vases, reflecting elements of them both in a 'compromise' position. Both vases have now contributed to a working surface (no longer a vessel), which lends itself to a new purpose, superseding the initial oppositional dilemma. When going through the metaphor animation process, symbols would avail themselves that generate novel options (such as building a mosaic table from broken pieces) to resolve ostensibly irreconcilable dilemmas or conflicts, which logic alone may not have achieved. This is because symbols work in a different currency – one of inspiration rather than perspiration; imagination rather than resignation. This process avails mental energy that would otherwise be tied up in the conflict of opposites, fueling the ego's futile

attempts to resolve the dilemma through logic and reasoning.

One could ponder the synthesis of opposites from the perspective of quantum physics, where the observer plays a key role in how something manifests, i.e. as a wave[9] *or* as a particle. The conscious mind definitely serves as an observer of its mental content, thereby altering *it* and with that, *itself*. The unconscious (defined as mental content outside immediate awareness) on the other hand is one where apparent opposites can 'co-exist' quite comfortably and productively, i.e. as *both* a wave *and* a particle (multiple realities or possibilities). In psychological terms one could therefore speak of *possibilities* (unconscious), which cease to be so when they become *actuality* (grasped consciously).

The symbols as transformational resources are special, as they by definition contain something hidden and tacit, which effectively is a sea of possibilities. One could visualize symbols which have not been fully animated as standing with their upper 'body' above the surface of the water (conscious: actual), with the rest of their body still submerged beneath the surface (unconscious: potential). This part is yet to be panned, like a gold miner would do in a creek, carefully distilling out the gold and letting the clutter wash away. The whole creek is full of potential and ever changing.

You will find that as you go through the animation process, secondary metaphors appear that also contain a wealth of growth potential. These also need to be animated to reveal their life-changing meaning.

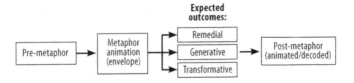

Figure 1.2: The metaphor animation process

An Invitation

For metaphor animation to serve you well, I am inviting you to strongly consider the following possibilities:

i. What you are aware of and identify as 'you' – the person you 'boot-up' in the morning, and don't need to reinvent – is not the whole you. Whilst familiar, and mostly resourceful, it is only the conscious part of 'you' that you are aware of. At best it is the dew drop on the leaf of the tree which is life. Its roots are buried in what Jung may call the 'Self'. This is where it gets its life-force/energy or libido, which is a collective fountain and not one in your psychological backyard. It is easy, however, to claim the fruits which may appear on the tree as of your own making as you stand proud, tall and self-aware, seemingly infallible, until the morning sun starts to give you perspective.

ii. If it is true that the conscious 'part' of you is merely the dew drop on the leaf of the tree which is life, then perhaps you need to start pondering as a real possibility the idea that you don't have all that much perspective. The ego, or organ of consciousness, simply doesn't know all that much (but thinks it does), and worse still, doesn't even know that much about *what it doesn't know*. This is quite a shaky position as the implications are that it thinks it knows a lot, whereas a whole chunk of that is based on simply not knowing what is really missing. This can become a recipe for disaster. Insisting that it does (a typical sign of 'ego') only worsens the situation when the old and wise creature called the 'Self' is waiting in the wings of the unconscious, and is willing to resolve even the most intractable problems. It, however, requires a simple acknowledgment by the ego that it is unable to come up with resolutions, as it does not have access to a bigger picture. Metaphor animation is that acknowledgment in action and the results show for themselves.

The Journey to Change through Metaphor Animation

By way of summary, you will be embarking on the following easy but powerful steps of metaphor animation. The steps will bring about the desired change/future scenario as embodied in the RGT metaphor:

Step 1: Converting negative narrative into metaphor

Converting a problem (be it past or present) into a metaphor is the first step. It galvanizes what can be lumpy issues into a solid and bounded frame. All that is required is to ask: 'What is my problem *LIKE*?' This should effortlessly and spontaneously evoke a metaphor which essentially means you are making a statement about a statement ('My life is *LIKE*'), which is the metaphor. The metaphor starts to act like a core that attracts and orders your thought patterns, rather than attending to the vague and undifferentiated problem. You will immediately realize that this is easier. If your issues are about, 'life' and you were to come up with the metaphor, 'My life sucks', then the latter is the donor domain and 'life' the beneficiary domain. There is something in the notion of 'sucks' which signifies matters around how you perceive your 'life'. From now on out, you will no longer be attending to your thoughts around an issue, but around the metaphor which captures it.

Step 2: Eliciting the transformative metaphor

People appear adept at spontaneously generating a metaphor that captures their challenges or problems. Staying within this negative frame, however, prevents solution-orientated thinking. Therefore, the next critical step is to generate the RGT metaphor. The distinction is drawn between these 'types' of positive metaphors to allow for a sliding scale based on your needs, but also to create a measurable, step-wise process. Transformation is located at the pinnacle, which would have meant that the animation process yielded highly growth-enhancing resource symbols. Eliciting a RGT metaphor creates the envelope or frame in which animation can happen. It is a key step as it paints a future desired scenario and, as a direction-setting resource, harnesses and focuses the animation process. Therefore it creates a focal point for the unconscious to direct its resource symbols, but also secures its commitment. The RGT metaphor contains all the facilitative material to achieve the change or transformation that you seek. In military terms one could speak of 'painting a target', which is the process of using a laser to direct an incoming missile (e.g. from a fighter jet) to a target. Simple questions help to elicit the RGT metaphor in response to the negative or problem metaphor that you first created. If you had said, 'My life sucks', ask, 'NOW, if my [INSERT WISH/DREAM/ASPIRATION HERE] were exactly as I want it to be, it would be LIKE...?'[10]

If you are seeking redemption from a past event that may be troubling you, ask the following metaphor eliciting question: 'NOW, if I had secured full release or redemption from X, Y or Z,[11] this would be LIKE...'[12] It is possible that you may experience the elicitation of a RGT metaphor as a step-wise process, i.e. that you begin with a metaphor precursor.[13] If, for example, you were to feel that you need to 'pull yourself together', this already is halfway to a metaphor, but it doesn't tell you 'LIKE WHAT'. Thus, the donor domain is missing. You would still have to ask: 'Pull myself together like what?' This may yield, 'Pull myself together like a blanket on a cold winter night.'

The RGT metaphor usually looks something like: 'If my life were exactly as I wish it to be, it would be like strawberries and cream.' It would be hard to argue that the prospect of 'strawberries and cream' as a tacit and symbolic representation signifying a future reality is significantly more motivating than working with 'My life sucks'. The positive donor domain ('strawberries and cream') sets the stage for the animation process, which will imbue the recipient domain with transformative energy as embodied in the resource symbols. There is one metaphor coined by Dale Carnegie which contains all the hallmarks of a RGT, and that is, 'When fate hands us a lemon, let's try to make lemonade.' Even though this may mean different things to different people the RGT metaphor, being top of mind, will channel thought patterns around, and fostered by, symbols to the desired metaphoric outcome – in this case lemonade.

What appears is that 'words' in the RGT metaphor (e.g. 'strawberries and cream', 'lemonade', etc.) are actually symbol precursors in that they set the stage for the resource symbols to emerge and manifest in the metaphor envelope. They are like Velcro which can attract its sticky unconscious counterparts (being resource symbols) to it. It is important to note that by symbols I don't mean 'things that stand for something else', like a heart on a product may stand for a healthy food choice. Within the context of metaphor animation, symbols are always converters of unconscious energy and an active function thereof.

For the moment, the RGT metaphor is static – you will be giving it the 'kiss of life' as you start animating, which is Step 3. Now, going forward, you will be dealing with the positive metaphor as a way to harness and channel your thoughts.

Step 3: Animating the transformative metaphor as a future reality

This step is the key to achieving the outcome or future reality implicit in the RGT metaphor – to achieve change or transformation right before your eyes. It brings the metaphor envelope to life and makes resource symbols proliferate and reveal their purpose. The focus shifts toward the unconscious mind, which is infinitely more resourceful than the conscious mind. It can supersede all current constraints and fulfill the desired future scenario as if it *already were real*. It is important to emphasize that your attitude is critical in attaining this future scenario. When you write down the RGT metaphor you need to adopt the attitude that its meaning (remediation, generative or transformative) and its riches are: (1) already known to you; and (2) manifest in your life. I have created a number of questions which will help you populate the metaphor envelope with symbols and help reveal their meanings/purpose.

The key questions to start out with are:

- 'What would be happening before my eyes as the RGT metaphor comes to life?'; and/or
- 'How would I know that the RGT metaphor is in motion/unfolding?'

For example, in the case of 'If life gives you lemons, try to make lemonade', you would ask: 'What is happening now that I am already making lemonade?' This should immediately yield a proliferation of symbols in addition to the precursors ('make lemonade'). Symbols may include lemons, sugar, a liquidizer, decanters, etc. Don't be misled into thinking that these are mere ingredients and utensils – they are symbols which harness and transpose unconscious energy for the purpose of remediation of a problem; offering generative solutions or complete transformation. The additional symbols and precursors can then be animated, using a number of *symbol-eliciting questions*, which range from *what* you experience through your senses (see; hear; feel) and *how* this appears to you (the quality of what you see, hear or feel). As part of this process you would fully inspect the metaphor envelope by inquiring about symbol typology (what types of symbols are evident); switching your position, e.g. from observer to participant; and determining if you are acting on the envelope and its symbols and further inspecting each of them. Also important and commensurate with the process of animation is to explore relationships between the symbols. These and other questions are elaborated further in Chapter 6. It would be best for you to draw your RGT metaphor and, by using arrows, show interrelationships. Further ordering would require a table format which is explained in Chapter 6 by way of an example. This table and drawing would help you clarify your insights and give you a sense as to how far the metaphor envelope has been animated.

You may have a sense that there are symbols which require further animation and/or that there may be resource symbols which have not yet availed themselves, resulting in further questions. My experience has shown that you may want to step away from the metaphor animation process and take a breather. You may find that further insights around symbols appear during this period of maturation.

A second round of symbol-animating questions has been included to help you intensify the animation process, thereby securing symbols that can transcend any polarities or seemingly insurmountable obstacles. This second round is aimed more at working with the 'how' (features) of the symbols, by applying 'meta-sensory editing processes' (explained later). This includes 'zooming in' (detail) and 'zooming out' (big picture); diminishing or enlarging symbols; exploring symbol typologies more in-depth, 'asking' symbols about their intent or purpose; exploring linkages between symbols; and 'shifting time' (day/night; past/present/future). After these steps you would have attained a highly fluid RGT metaphor – one which is no longer static, but animated and full of life. It is also likely that, at this point, the animation process would have thrown up some real nettles in the form of oppositional dilemmas; conflicts or other polarities. These can include internal strife ('I'm in two minds') or facing external choices, which are oppositional ('If I go with X, the outcome is undesirable'; 'If I go with Y, the outcome is undesirable; now I'm stuck and in a hiatus'). This is when the ego would have hit a wall and is no longer able to reconcile the polarities. Symbols are required to transcend them and bring clarity, insight, emotional relief and resolution.

Resolution of polarities at the brink of transformation

It is true that a breakdown is a breakthrough, loaded with potential. Oppositional dilemmas are 'mental rim territory' – the edge between continent and sea, where the mental vehicles you have used thus far become patently obsolete and unable to meet 'ocean-going requirements' (or vice versa). The animation process is mostly going to take you to the brink of becoming unstuck/feeling stuck – with options before you not yielding the outcomes you desire. You have to reinvent yourself. Unconscious resources as yielded through symbols are critical to enable this. Chapter 7 aims to give you a firmer grasp on the psychological dynamics underlying oppositional dilemmas. You may feel a resistance toward the scenario painted in the RGT metaphor, even though it is clearly mind-expanding. Equipped with this insight and awareness about oppositional dilemmas, you will be able to apply the symbol animation resources more effectively to hasten progression toward transformation.

Up to now, you may have achieved a sense of remediation of a problem, or attainment of a generative scenario such as a wish. Yet, you may want something more profound. Transformation will bring about lasting and profound changes, if not an epiphany.

Equipped with the above certainty, be patient, prepare, and prepare to be amazed!

ENDNOTES

1   Metaphor Animation for Personal Transformation (M.A.P.T) ('The Brügge Method') is the methodology I developed for this book. (Explained in detail later).

2   Mental filters which we apply to make sense of what we experience and which direct our ordinary thoughts in a habitual manner. (Explained more in depth later.)

3   Tacey, 2006.

4   Spelled like this, trans-*phor*-mation reflects the inherent power of the positively stated or RGT (Remedial, Generative and Transformative) Metaphor: meta*phor* that transforms.

5   This means that the brain remains malleable and can rewire itself. Formation of new memories through learning (notably complex tasks) is an example of such plasticity as it results in alterations in the contact points (synapses) of nerve cells and their connection with others.

6   An envelope of envelopes is a frame around metaphoric envelopes, as the animation process could yield symbols, insights and possibilities beyond one envelope.

7   The ego is both subject and object. The subjective part is the sense you have of who you are. The objective part is being aware of this sense of who you are. You can therefore 'look' at the ego from the 'outside' perspective and observe its 'ways'.

8   The unconscious contains psychological material that is currently outside conscious awareness. Carl Jung added a second layer, the collective unconscious. Symbols are likely to emerge there and become personalized in shape and character once you become consciously aware of, and

engage with it.

9 'Wave and particle' are merely used as an example from quantum physics to demonstrate that for the unconscious mind the 'world is our oyster', and that many realities exist. It is the conscious mind (observation) which prunes these into a select few.

10 Strictly speaking, the presence of 'like' denotes a simile (a figure of speech whereby unrelated things are compared). However, I found that the presence of 'like' is necessary to elicit metaphor in a very specific manner. The question, 'How is your life?', would have produced a number of general descriptions such as, 'My life is OK'; 'My life is great', etc. rather than a proper metaphor, even if the presence of a 'like' in the sentence by definition is a simile. If the word 'like' is removed, a metaphor still remains, e.g. 'My life is (like) a rainbow.'

11 X, Y or Z could be 'guilt, fear, shame or anger, relating to an event in my life where I/someone else did/said...'

12 This may yield, 'This would be like a weight off my shoulders.' This positive metaphor then needs to be animated further.

13 Note: this is different from the symbol *precursors*.

Chapter 2

The Magic of Metaphor

I am like the leader of a group of pillaging Huns.
Corporate executive

Memories, thoughts and emotions can be a bewildering flurry of information and often confusing and hard to make sense of. Metaphors help organize this information (as represented in our ordinary thoughts[1] about reality) by 'applying' filters, which color what we experience. (Just think of rose-colored glasses). This 'ability' of metaphors is hinted at by the word element 'meta-' (meaning over, above or beyond) in that metaphors are 'higher up' in our mental landscape than ordinary thoughts. By way of proper definition, metaphor means that an idea, action or object is described in a manner normally referring to something else, e.g. 'He froze' would mean that the person's behavior is described as if it were ice. The characteristics of the one (ice) is carried over to the other (person's action/inaction) so that the second is referred to as if it were the first. This is in accordance with the Greek origins of *metaphor* (*metaphora*), whereby *meta-* means 'over' and *-pherein* means 'to carry' – 'to carry over'.

Therefore, metaphors can be seen as meta-cognitive[2] programs or drivers which alter the manner in which we receive and attend to 'reality'[3] through our senses and thoughts. In so doing, our feelings and emotions also change. If we, using the above example, look at a person's behavior using metaphor, this significantly alters the meaning we attribute to what they are doing. This is much richer than simply saying, 'the person stopped moving'.

It therefore makes sense to work with metaphors rather than to get into the 'substance' of our thoughts, worries and emotions. To accept this as a premise, however, you need to accept as *fundamental* the idea that you don't ever attend to 'reality' itself, but only your *experience* of it. Therefore, there exists a gap between your experience or map of reality and reality itself. Metaphors imbue our experiences with meaning by shaping how we *attend to information* and *how we react to it*. In so doing, they seek to reduce that gap, thus enriching our experiences, albeit imperfectly. Inevitably, some information is lost or altered by this process of selectively attending to our experiences. This is much like sculpting: in order to bring forth a beautiful sculpture, much of the raw material from which it is derived must be carved or chiseled away. This analogy points to another inherent characteristic of metaphors – they reflect that which is (the raw material; the actual) and that which can be (the sculpture; potential). When we work with our metaphors and their building blocks, our experience of reality inevitably will also change. This is much easier than to get stuck in the mental narrative which feeds on itself, gets more complex and often does not lead to a resolution. As you will become aware in the next chapters, metaphor simplifies, clarifies and enlightens. Metaphors are one of the most powerful ways to present the workings of our own consciousness to us in a comprehensive manner. Furthermore, they are emotionally highly evocative and contain a high emotional 'charge', like a fire cracker, waiting for its fuse to be lit. Just ponder the following: "I was so exhausted, it felt like molten lava had been poured into my legs and solidified there".

Lengthening Your Mental 'Coastline'
In order to fully grasp the power of metaphor, do the following:

- Take two pieces of A4 paper;

- Take the first piece of paper, make a fist and place it on the paper, then draw the outline of your fist, using a pen or pencil.
- Take the second paper and put your hand on it flat (fingers extended; palm facing down). Then draw an outline of your open hand.
- Now get yourself some string, wool or dental floss and a glue stick. Stick the string loosely onto the outlines of your fist and hand, respectively.
- Once you have done this, pull the strings off the two papers before the glue has dried.
- Place the two pieces of string next to each other.

What are you noticing? The piece of string that you used to trace the outlines of your open hand should be significantly longer than that of your fist. The short string (fist) represents the metaphor *pre*-animation. The long string (open hand) represents the metaphor, *post*-animation. You have effectively lengthened the coastline of your mind: creating long stretches of foreshore (your extended fingers) with little alcoves (the space at the bottom between your fingers). Now you have a phenomenal view and perspective on your needs and aspirations, no matter where you are positioned. In the case of your fist, the foreshore is a lot shorter, constraining your view.

The animation process is the progression from fist to open hand; from limited perspective to a wealth of information and insight. Metaphor elicits raw information about our mental coastline as a totality, providing a coherent, albeit compact picture of meanings that can be further unpacked. Ordinary thoughts on the other hand only provide snippets of information that have to be dealt with one by one, trying to achieve a whole from the parts. This does not make sense, as the parts derive their meaning from the whole, even though they help shape it. Metaphor is like a 'zipped' computer file. The file name is all we have as an indication of the contents. Once we 'unzip all' (animation of the metaphor), we have a wealth of information becoming available to foster an understanding of 'us' and our future potential.

It is more fruitful to work with metaphor as it is reflective of the penthouse suite of our mental 'building'. It provides an already rich, panoramic view of our experiential world and how we represent this to ourselves through words. The floors below have progressively more constrained views, never achieving a total picture. If we consider the metaphors we so readily come up with, it becomes evident how they reflect more or less everything we are and deal with as human beings.

Your Brain's Constraints in Dealing with Information

According to Miller (1956), human short-term memory and judgment is constrained by what he calls the 'magical number 7, plus or minus 2'. In other words, we are constrained by the amount of information that we can process and attend to at any given time. The findings by Miller have received criticism because humans in general (and a few in a gifted way) are able to extend their memory span through so-called 'chunking'. Chunking refers to the grouping of information as a picture(s) or narrative. One can chunk 'up' to the more general or even abstract, or 'down' to the specific/concrete. When I worked in the field of neuropsychology, I often observed people whose memory I assessed, grouping information as a story. If that which had to be memorized and recalled included word lists, they would typically generate a story (chunking information 'up'), during the learning process. This story served as a bounded and coherent frame or context, which significantly aided the recall of the words forming part of it, later. The stories worked so effectively that I ended up also recalling them and the words, to this day. One person generated a story out of words which included 'moon', 'farmer', 'curtain', etc. Stringing these together yielded a story: 'When the *moon* came out, the *farmer* opened the *curtain*...' As an 'envelope' of sorts, learning the story rather than the words spared mental resources, overcoming processing constraints. The story, being a sequence of events, also facilitated recall of individual words much more readily than trying to bring them each to mind separately (a process that is mentally more resource intensive).

Metaphor circumvents the '7 plus or minus 2' dilemma in a similar fashion, organizing information (thoughts; feelings; experiences) in a coherent and compact fashion by transferring notions about a donor domain to a recipient domain, conveying some meaning to the person having generated the metaphor. Pregnant with meaning as they are, metaphors however carry tacit meanings too, which need to be unpacked. Most of the real meaning of metaphor in fact is more than meets the eye. The steps for drilling down to the core of the tacit meaning of metaphor (where its true insight-generating elixir is located) are the subject of this chapter.

How Metaphors Are Put Together

A metaphor derives its meaning from its entirety; from its *Gestalt* or coherent totality. However, it comprises various sub-components called *symbols*. The symbols are change agents that are launched from the unconscious mind, but only reveal some aspects of what/who they are (if we can give them human characteristics for a moment). They always retain a hidden element – something that is alluded to or signified, but requires animation to reveal its essence and with that, provide the new perspective to resolve issues. It is crucially important to understand right away that a symbol in the context of this book is not something that 'stands for something else', e.g. like a diamond may be the symbol of permanence or strength. Neither are symbols as used here necessarily universal, i.e. that they have 'objective' meaning or power independent of the person using them. However, it may be possible that your symbols have a mythological background. It is important to accept that symbols are loaded with meaning and potential based on your personal circumstances, experiences and aspirations. It is the *process* of symbols making their way from your unconscious into your conscious mind, and the color they derive from the dynamics of your mind and personality, that make them salient. Consequently, what is important is that symbols as processes are more important than symbols as 'things'. When they are known fully, they lose their characteristics as symbols and become objects.

Similarly, a metaphor certainly does not contain all its symbols right away. Look for example at the following: *'He flies by the seat of his pants.'* There are some potential symbols in the metaphor, e.g. 'flying' and 'seat of his pants'. This potentially refers to the human in question making plans as they were going along.[4] I say 'potentially' because only the person using the metaphor will be able to elicit the meaning of the symbols, as these and their transformative power are subjective and contextual. I therefore call that which appears in the metaphor overtly (but doesn't reveal its meaning), *symbol precursors*. (A *precursor* is one that alludes to, or announces something else). These components of metaphor precede the actual symbols, and 'warm' their seats or create molds or receptacles for them, which the animation process will help populate by bringing the symbols into consciousness, revealing their actual meaning. In the case of the above, there may be no airplane at all and 'seat of pants' may reveal something else. Remember that this book will teach you how to convert the metaphor that depicts a current state of mind that is undesirable into a positive mindset. In this positive metaphor, symbol precursors also appear which need to be worked with. This is the subject of the forthcoming chapters.

Think of the symbols, as sub-components of metaphor, as the strands of a spider web. They are interconnected, so that when one strand/part (or sub-component) of the web is disturbed, this disturbance reverberates throughout. Some of these disturbances may be felt more strongly in the immediate vicinity of the impact and taper off, being felt a little less in the remote reaches of the web. These disturbances would alter the *structure* of the web, e.g. by strands being stretched or pulled out of alignment. However, the way in which the web is organized and its functionality as a whole is maintained. A slightly disheveled spider web is a spider web no less. We would still recognize it and not call it something else, as long as its total look is preserved. This is much like the face of Mr Potatohead in the *Toy Story* movies – even as he loses his eyes, ears and nose (a disturbance), the overall organization of his face prevails. Even as his eyes, ears, nose or mouth land in the wrong places, they still make up a face, as my daughter's Frankenstein-esque experiments have shown. The very characteristics of the web determine which disturbances are felt and how. For example, a web with widely spaced strands would be perfect to catch large insects, but would let smaller ones through. These types of bugs would never interact with the web and thus never impact its structure. A web with more fragile strands would catch small insects, but could break when impacted by large insects. Here the structure of the web and how it responds and the nature of the impact (a big bug) could potentially create catastrophic failure or necessitate repair. If the web is merely broken in places, it can be repaired or components replaced, thus ensuring its functionality. However, the repaired sections of the web might be less flexible, thus influencing the structure of the web, how it responds to disturbances as a whole and its breaking point. If the web were to become strained or taut due to a change in its structure over time, taking it to the edge of its operational 'design specifications', progressively smaller impacts (bug disturbances) would be required. Then, finally, it will take the 'last straw to break the camel's back'.

How is the analogy of a spider web similar to metaphor and how is this important?

i.   Much like a spider web, the building blocks of individual metaphors are linked to each other, creating a system. The whole is more than the sum total of its parts. If various spider webs were to be interconnected to cover a big area, this would be a system of spider webs. If various metaphors are interconnected, a metaphor system of systems is created, with each system influencing the others and its sub-components. Changes in the components affect the system as a whole and how it responds to triggers from the environment. Small changes (flexibility; replacement/repair/remediation of components) are adaptive and necessary and ensure the organizational integrity of the system as a whole and its survival, allowing productive interaction with the environment. If, however, the system becomes too rigid and it is unable to recover (to go back to baseline or a resting position, like a spider web), then a small impact can disturb its structure or even its total organization. The system is then unable to stay in a productive and functional spectrum of interaction with the environment. Then a new system must emerge.

ii. The metaphors we use are an uncannily accurate reflection of how we experience our lives, what we think and feel and how we react. Flexible metaphor will result in, or be indicative of flexible thoughts, emotions and behaviors. Rigid metaphor, on the other hand, will be the converse. This book will show you how to keep yourself flexible mentally by engaging and unpacking your remedial, generative or transformative metaphors. If your metaphors, as an accurate reflection of your headspace, are already rigid and on the edge of their functional range, small insights can have a dramatic effect. This would be like the structure of the main strands of the mental spider web changing, resulting in a collapse and replacement of the web. Some of the remaining strands may be used as building blocks for the new web. As a mirror of our minds, dramatic transformation through working with metaphor can ensue.

iii. Much like the spacing of the strands in the spider web, catching some but not all bugs, the nature of the metaphor would determine whether and how we (like the spider) perceive information (the bug flying into the web), and how this influences our thoughts, emotions and behavior. Metaphor does not only direct our thoughts and feelings to environmental triggers for inspection, it also provides some of the raw material to make sense of them. This is much like the web which is triggered by a bug, providing the spider with the 'food' and 'raw information' (strong or weak vibrations) about its characteristics, e.g. whether the bug is big or small. The spider has to do further 'work' (e.g. cocooning) to 'process' the bug and benefit from it. Similarly, metaphors and their sub-components have to be processed further to create a more comprehensive and useful model about our lives and to maximize their benefit in making sense and identifying patterns. Whilst some metaphors are more revealing than others, all are implicit in terms of the information they carry and the resources they contain to foster change and transformation. They first have to be decoded.

iv. If we change our system of metaphors or the sub-components of the metaphors we use, the manner in which we deal with our experiences will change too.

Being imbued with meaning from the collective unconscious

through transformative symbols, the metaphor spider web's strands are not tethered to tree branches, but beyond to connect us to the life force.

Coming to Your Senses

The building blocks of the symbols (S) contained in metaphor interrelate to make up the whole (see overlapping area in the Figure below) and enable its meaning to be conveyed to you as the beneficiary. The most noticeable aspect of metaphors is that its symbols often include sensory information, being visual, auditory, and kinesthetic, taste or smell. These sights, sounds, taste and smells help us *access* (in the case of metaphor in memory) or *construct* (in the case of deeply personal, novel metaphor) that which is *our* metaphor (and its symbols) to depict what we think, feel, plan, or have done. Feldman (2006) notes that the 'metaphor system is grounded in the body in terms of the primary metaphors. In each primary metaphor such as "affection is warmth" an experience brings together a subjective judgment (here, affection) and a sensory-motor occurrence (temperature)' (p.200). Metaphor therefore spans our whole being – it is embodied.

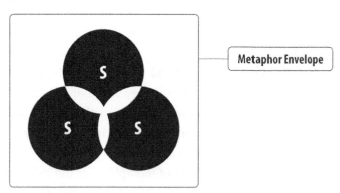

Figure 2.1: Symbols are interrelated within the metaphor envelope

If we work with the sensory information, we already start to explore and deepen our metaphor landscape, taking us outside the domain of mere words, which as labels and based on past experience, constrain and obscure the total meaning, availing only face value. When we start altering our sensory impressions contained in our metaphors, we apply active meta-sensory[5] filters, thus changing how the metaphor is put together and with that the contents as well as the entire meaning. We are like Robin Williams in the sci-fi film *Final Cut*, who as a 'cutter' edits out after-death memory implants that have recorded all moments of a person's life. Undesirable events are 'cut' and a spliced version of the person's life is shown at a commemorative ceremony, called 'Rememory'. This brings the family of the deceased great comfort, as their passed loved one is portrayed positively, minus their shadows (their disowned uncouth traits and behaviors). When we attend to our metaphors, we become 'cutters' of memories of our experiences (or the metaphor itself), 'post-mortem'. If the metaphor relates to the past, the event which it seeks to portray has transpired – we can never travel back in time and change it. Going forward, however, we can work with the metaphor. As we start changing and enriching it, our memories, expectations and future behavior also change.

What you see (Visual)

Think of the metaphor, 'being between a rock and a hard place'. The symbols making up this metaphor evoke strong visual notions, being the presence of at least one rock, and a yet to be

"The Rock" ⟶   X ⟵ "A Hard Place"

Figure 2.2: In-between a 'rock' and a 'hard place'

identified element called a 'hard place', with a person evidently being wedged in-between. Similar is the metaphor, 'light at the end of the tunnel': both the tunnel and the light are visual.

We can apply meta-sensory filters by inspecting the more detailed visual sensory elements of our metaphors, thus gathering richer information about our subjective experiences. If we apply meta-sensory filters, and alter some of the following so-called sub-sensory qualities of the metaphor symbols, we will augment or change the meaning of the metaphor and with that, our subjective experience, whether memorized or 'live/on-line':

- FAST or slow movement in metaphor;
- STILLS vs. movie-like metaphor;
- LIGHT or dark features of metaphor;
- FRAMED or panoramic metaphor; and
- CLOSE or distant metaphor.

Research shows that 80% of our experiences are made sense of visually. A significant amount of our brain power is dedicated to processing visual samples of our encounters with 'reality'. The latter is a subjective construction; the world 'out there' serving as a mere trigger or prompt for our nervous system to start making sense or meaning about what it encounters. It is little wonder then that metaphors as internal processes are generally visual in nature. It is a lot easier (and quicker) in terms of neural processes in the brain to deal with pictures; words take a lot longer to avail themselves. It is easier to recall the name of something memorized previously if we are shown a picture of it (this is called recognition memory).

What you hear (Auditory)
'She is wearing a *loud* dress' is an interesting example of an auditory donor characteristic (noise) being superimposed on a recipient object, probably referring to bright colors, but without mentioning

them. For the user of the metaphor, there was something more evocative in a word related to noise rather than color. An alternative could have been 'The dress looks like a jumble.'

What you feel/sense (Kinesthetic)

'This job is like pushing water uphill' is an example of a metaphor with kinesthetic essence ('pushing'). The donor domain ('pushing water') here conveys something essential to the user about the beneficiary domain ('job'). Another example would be, 'As we leave the urban area and enter the countryside, I can just feel the *tension rolling off of me*.' Metaphor can also draw on inner sensations (proprioception) to bring its point across, e.g. 'An empty stomach has no ears' (illegal pit diamond miner interviewed on TV).

Words

Words are the building blocks of many metaphors. They are 'higher up' in our mental *hie*rarchy (see next section), since words constrain how we perceive our world and structure our experiences. Whilst they help us access associations and attend to certain meanings and past experiences, they also draw our attention away from others and our sensory experiences. This is simply because experiences that have been labeled with words more easily attract our attention and over time, through repetition, those experiences are represented to our mind's eye more readily than unlabeled ones. Experiencing through our senses (as opposed to *representing* labeled experiences) is therefore constrained through words. The latter can never fully capture pure, 'unlabeled' experience. In order to be 'freed' from the constraints of labels (content), much attention has to be paid to unpacking the sensory experience (sub-sensory structure and relationships), using meta-sensory filters or drivers. Einstein said that most of his seminal ideas came to him as images, free from the shackles of words. Edelman and Tononi (2000) confirm that 'at every instant, the brain goes far beyond the information given...a sharp distinction between transmission and storage in the brain starts to vanish' (p.138). Working with the sensory experiences frees up problem-solving potential, facilitates inflow of problem-solving information from the unconscious, and harnesses the imagination with the view to that which is yet to materialize. *Metaphor animation is your high-road into the arena of sensory experience. Curiosity is your access pass.* Whatever the symbols that the animation process yields are called is secondary to the meaning they have for you. By the time you have named them, they are close to having lost what qualifies them as symbols, namely their transformative and insight-generating power. Then, they become mere things. (The table below shows the animation focal points. You will note that daily

	METAPHOR PRE-CURSOR	Metaphor put in negative terms	Conversion into positive metaphor	Animation Focal points:
METAPHORIC STREAM (whole representation)	"Things aren't working out for me"	"My life is aimlessly wandering"	"My life is like plain sailing"	✘
Sensory stream (part- experiential):				✔
• *What* we see (visual)				✔
• *What* we hear (auditory)				✔
• *What* we feel (kinesthetic)				✔
Sub-sensory stream (part-experiential):				✔
• *How* we see				✔
• *How* we hear				✔
• *How* we feel				✔
Conceptual stream (daily narrative) (part representation)				✘

Table 2.1: Summary of animation touch-points

narrative is excluded, as from now on out, only the metaphor is engaged with.)

The Uncanny Power of Metaphor

The mind seems to be able to come up with novel/personal[6] or common/colloquial metaphor[7] at will and at the drop of a hat, so to speak. I observed this in myself and many of the people I have coached, inspiring me to explore this seemingly universal human tendency[8] (which turns out to be a transformative resource), further.

The spontaneous generation of metaphor in response to personal issues or thoughts to self or in discussion with others is so rapid that it appears to involve little participation by the conscious mind. The latter in fact seems to be an often surprised observer rather than an active participant and has little to offer by way of suggestions for improvements. The metaphor that emerges is able to accurately and compactly capture and transfer onto the beneficiary domain, key raw data which will become the subject of the animation process explained in detail later.

Metaphor Envelope, Composition and Process

Applying the pyramid idea to issues around faith and the metaphor, *'My faith is solid like a rock'*, the following is evident (refer to Figures 2.3 and 2.4 below):

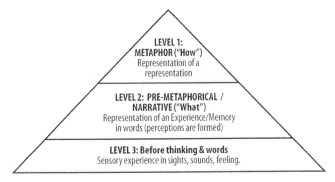

Figure 2.3: Metaphor structure and process

i.   Level 3: This captures the experience in sensory terms (perhaps visual and kinesthetic) and intuitive terms, before words as arbitrary labels are attached to it. At the very periphery (starting point) of processing by our nervous system, sensory experiences are pre-conscious[9] and pre-verbal, that is, they have not yet entered consciousness and we have not captured them in a web of words. This does not mean that snippets of images and sounds may not become visible on our 'mental screen' as impressions and start coalescing into a recognizable form without words. However, language helps us make sense of this inflow of sensory information by relating it to past experience (held in memory) or helps to construct a new scenario that we can then attach a new descriptive label to. Unlike an ordinary sentence, the metaphors we come up with are uniquely coherent and organized as well as definitive in the manner in which they are able to express our thoughts, feelings, issues and desires. Some metaphors are exceptionally sensory[10] (rather than strongly conceptual: level 2), in their organization. These include: 'This job is a *tall* order' (visual experience); 'I was so angry, I was simmering inside' (kinesthetic/proprioceptive experience); or 'It struck a note with me' (auditory experience). Altering the metaphor at the sensory level (see meta-sensory editing process in Chapter 6) will also change it and with that our experience, as tinkering with the parts (as building blocks) will affect the whole metaphor. With that, the subjective meaning of the metaphor will also start to change as well as our experiences as expressed in ordinary thoughts or words. This will start the process of achieving remedial, generative or transformative outcomes.

ii. Level 2: This captures what the issue, challenge or

experience is about or specifically relates to (representing the experience to ourselves). Language helps us to do a 'search function' through our mind. This helps us access parts of our personal or shared history which would help us articulate our sensory experience and identify what we mean in respect of a challenge or need. Language also helps us to make information more readily available to conscious thought. This is referred to as the 'what' (with the focus on the recipient domain), but is *pre-metaphorical* because the critical overlay of the donor domain ('how') has not yet happened. It is a critical step, however, as metaphor can be more readily distilled when words exist, rather than just sensory 'information'. Level 2 sets a frame or conceptually bounded envelope(s) and keeps other information at bay that does not fit into the meaning-creating domain or definition of what has to be dealt with via the metaphor.

iii. Level 1: by eliciting metaphor at the highest level – 'meta' (above and beyond[11]) – we create a *re-presentation* (metaphor) *of a re-presentation* (experience and day-to-day representation thereof in words). This is where a meta-domain (donor notions) is superimposed on, and starts the process of clarifying the recipient domain[12]. If you were to say, 'My faith is solid, like a rock', this would be:

- 'how': the description ('like a rock') (Level 1); about
- 'what': the narrative (pre-metaphorical: 'faith') (Level 2); about
- 'it': your experience (before words / unlabeled) (Level 3).

Enlightening as it is, the metaphor is 'commenting' by virtue of its greater clarity or intelligence on your narrative and your experience of faith, and helps qualify it, by comparing it to a solid rock. Remember: metaphor transfers meaning from the one to the other (rock to faith). This introduces the key characteristic of metaphor, namely *'how?'* ('like a solid rock'). This metaphor, if personal (rather than universal/colloquial), is constructed by the unconscious and may be entirely novel. No prior knowledge exists and language is merely used to put it together as a unique notion and sequence of words, thus solidifying its intended meaning for the user. Sometimes, common metaphor such as 'I have my head in the clouds' is also used, as the user perceives it to be essentially sufficiently rich to capture the intended meaning. This may be more expedient, although the generation of a unique metaphor appears as swift and effortless, but above all, highly resonant at a personal level.

The 'like' (whether explicit or implied) does not only complete the metaphor, it also often contains sub-sensory statements, further qualifying the donor domain. The *'how'* (characteristics of the rock) more than the 'what' (rock as noun) qualifies our faith – a porous rock may have created doubt as to our faith.

Hence, Level 1 ('how') is stacked above the 'what' (Level 2). For example, a rock, an essentially arbitrary label for something hard, if further unpacked may evoke:

- A *picture* of a *big* rock (visual: rock; sub-sensory: big). Visualizing a big rock rather than a pebble may give more certainty and provide a foundation for faith. (This is completely subjective though: for another person the metaphor animation process may yield a pebble that can skip over the water or rest at the bottom of a brook, e.g. 'My faith is resilient, like a pebble.')
- Something tactile (kinesthetic; sub-sensory: hard rather than soft/porous).

The 'sub-sensory qualities' or building blocks of the rock arise from Level 3. 'Sub-sensory' (meaning underneath our sensory experiences) are the characteristics or finer grain of what we experience through our senses, including various colors/black and white. Once we name these qualities, they would have become conscious and subjected to the process of making meaning of it (through animation), including by tagging it so that we can communicate with others about our experience.

Figure 2.4: Metaphor composition and process: Example

When you go through the next steps, you should start noticing that you can work with metaphor building blocks (contained in Level 1) at the sub-sensory level (Level 3) (before words). By altering the mental filters (being the sub-sensory components) (how you see; hear; feel; taste and smell), through meta-sensory editing work (e.g. changing 'hard' to 'soft'), the meaning of the metaphor and, with that, your day-to-day experience and narrative is altered too. If the work is done correctly, we should experience change or at least relief (the 'remedial' aspect of metaphor animation).

The key to hierarchal layering, therefore is that the over-arching always defines and qualifies (positive or negative) the underlying. Just think of 'meta'- (meaning above and beyond) in metaphor as the *donor domain* part (that which is 'given', e.g. 'solid rock'). This always defines the *recipient domain* part, as we can engage better with an issue if we have the benefit of the intelligence and enlightenment of the donor domain. The donor domain brings order to our thoughts and feelings. Quite by chance I discovered that two anagrams of 'meta' are 'team' and 'tame'. Both are true for the role of metaphor in our lives. It helps us 'tame' our thoughts and we work together with it in a 'team'. Much work, however, has to be done as the metaphor still needs to be unpacked and enriched to yield results and resolution. This never works the other way round as the recipient domain cannot define or enlighten the donor domain, only vice versa. A metaphor such as 'My rock is solid like a faith' simply doesn't make sense.

The key issue to be remembered about the levels is that you *no longer attend directly to your experience* (as 'represented' through words/senses[13]), but to a re-presentation of that representation, being the metaphor. It follows, within the context of a specific issue illuminated by the metaphor, that if the latter changes, your experience and how you talk about it in day-to-day language and your behavior will also change. This reflects the sheer brilliance and force of metaphor as an unconscious resource.

The following figure clarifies things further. It has been shown that as 'information' from our eyes, for example, progresses through our brains to the visual cortex at the back and then forward to the frontal lobes (conscious awareness) (see vertical arrows), feed*back* loops ensure that all progressive (forward) stages communicate back to the earliest stages of information processing. In so doing, these earliest (and perhaps most elementary or coarsely grained) stages of information processing are kept 'up to speed' (thin horizontal feedback arrows) about what is 'happening' in the more advanced stages, where information is starting to coalesce and being related/compared to memories of past experience. In so doing, what we already know (so-called top-down processing) informs and constrains what is currently being experienced (bottom-up processing). The converse is also true in that feed-*forward* streams also keep the forthcoming information stages informed of what is about to happen, thereby also altering the structure of our experience. This is why what we experience always seems current, even though what we become aware of is actually already 'old' (a few hundred milliseconds), and a mishmash of our memories and current experience. That is why neuroscientist and Nobel Prize winner Gerald Edelman refers to what we experience as the 'remembered present'.

As we consciously attend to what we experience by working with our metaphors and their sub-components or symbols, we make a marked impact on what is happening in our sensory 'periphery' and how information from our senses is attended to. Metaphor structures the processes of attending to our experiences, accentuating some, and blotting out others. Metaphor therefore also is a form of selective attention. Symbols (nuanced at a sub-sensory level: how they look; what we hear, feel, taste or smell) and their meaning, derived from the whole, strongly color and manipulate what we experience. This is a good thing, as it frees us from the dictates of our 'reality'. By attending (applying conscious thought) to our metaphors *about* our reality, we can alter it at will (see arrow pointing to the right). We are no longer the victims of our 'reality'. However what we cling to as 'true' (even our metaphors) only seems real because it has been aggregated from our lived experience and contains an associated emotional tone. This does not, however, make it true, even if we have invested heavily in making sense of things around us. It remains a pervasive and convincing illusion.

Again, there is something positive here: if our metaphors are only a subjective version of the truth, we should be willing to work with them and alter them, and by changing them as truths we also change our thoughts and how we experience the world. In the words of Wayne Dwyer: 'When we change the way we look at things, the things we look at change.'

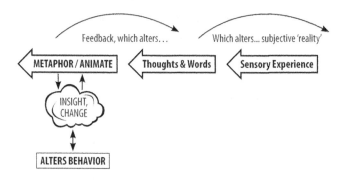

Figure 2.5: How metaphor brings about change

Summary

✓ Our ability to spontaneously generate metaphors is quite uncanny – they pop into our heads with little by way of conscious participation or effort.

✓ Metaphors bring order to our thoughts and emotions, thereby helping us make sense of them. They help us tap into a vast unconscious resource base that we can't grasp or account for. We are always privy to the outcome (insight), never how our mind has achieved a certain feat – herein vests the magic. We need to believe in what we *don't* see. Speaking of belief: the belief that metaphor has the power to transform unlocks this phenomenon.

✓ Metaphors help us overcome the information processing constraints of our conscious mind and help us extend the 'coastline' of our mental landscape/headspace. They do so by organizing what we experience (either from our own memories or 'the environment') in a coherent and compact fashion. However, they always contain hidden meanings that, when animated, reveal themselves. In fact, the larger part of metaphors – that which they allude to; new associations – exists outside conscious awareness.

✓ Metaphors are higher-order or more abstract representations of our thoughts, memories and how/what we perceive through our senses (that which we so readily call 'reality'). As a 'representation of a representation' (of words and sensory 'information') they are infinitely richer[14] than mere words strung together. Being higher order, they are powerful meaning-making filters. It therefore makes sense to attend to our metaphors as instruments for change rather than to our 'ordinary' thoughts. As we enrich and animate our RGT metaphors, our thoughts about what is 'real' for us change quite dramatically and with that, our emotions. Transformative (positive) metaphor will have a positive impact on our emotions and general well-being.

✓ Being a representation of a representation, metaphors contain donor notions that clarify recipient notions. For example, the former would be the part usually starting with 'like', e.g. 'Life is like a park bench.' 'Life' is the recipient domain as it benefits from the clarity implied by 'park bench'. The latter, however, has to be animated to release resource symbols which will aid in the transformative, remedial or generative process that you are pursuing. It is about maximizing the meaning, both explicit and implicit.

✓ RGT metaphors don't only reveal actuality, they reveal potentiality. They help us visualize and concretize a highly desirable future by creating a 'glide-path' for our thought patterns and behavior to attain that future – NOW. In this sense, metaphors are a *history of your future*.

✓ RGT metaphor helps harness and focus unconscious resources, thereby strengthening our egos and enabling us to see life in a crisp and fresh way; restoring hope and optimism and unleashing a deep wellspring of motivation.

✓ Metaphors derive their coherence from their *Gestalt* (the organization of their totality), which is 'more' (and more profound) than the sub-components which comprise it. I have used the analogy of a spider web to explain this. Perturbations/changes at the level of the symbols comprising the metaphor reverberate through the whole metaphor and alter it, whilst sustaining its organization. Being so deeply reflective of our inner lives (that which is known and not known), metaphors – when we animate them – are like magic mirrors: they alter us when we look into them. If we don't transform negative metaphor into generative metaphor through animation, the negative metaphors ratify our inner lives, rather than help us change. Simply put, by changing metaphors as richly textured pictures of what and who we are, rather than dealing with the flurry that is our ordinary thoughts, we can change ourselves. Animated metaphors reflexively alter our thoughts, emotions and underlying neural fabric (our brains) which are able to continually grow and renew.

✓ At its core, a metaphor is exceptionally sensory (consisting of what we hear; see; feel; taste or smell). As building blocks or foundation stones, engaging with the symbols that make up the metaphor alters it as a whole. When we attach words to symbols they only serve as arbitrary labels to categorize them and communicate them to others.

✓ Metaphors, once animated, are high-powered transformative catalysts. Metaphors allow you to no longer attend directly to your experience, but a representation (the metaphor) of a representation (your sensory experiences and words as labels for them). This will free you from the dictates of what you may readily accept as your unalterable 'reality'.

ENDNOTES

1   By this I mean thoughts that drift in and out of conscious awareness without taking the shape of metaphors.

2   Meta-programs are deep-rooted and often unconscious, content-free programs or strategies that we use to make sense of and manipulate our thought patterns and with that the manner in which we deal with information and the way in which we behave. Focusing on the 'big picture' rather than detail are examples of meta-programs. A person looking at the big picture would describe a scene differently from a person being attentive to detail. As the originators of Neuro Linguistic Programming (NLP), Richard Bandler and John Grinder have shown, reducing the size of a disturbing picture tends to reduce its emotional impact. The converse is true if pictures associated with positive experiences are enlarged in our mind's eye.

3   You will note that 'reality' always appears in inverted commas, as for 'our reality' to manifest, it requires our active participation. We shape it, and are shaped by it.

4   The general meaning is well known, i.e. to determine a course of action on the spur of the moment, rather than ahead of time; to take a risk.

5   Meta-sensory means above and beyond the sensory [visual; hearing; kinesthetic (touch); olfactory (smell); and gustatory (taste)] and, being positioned and applied like this, can alter the sensory experiences which shape our memories, memories of emotions and emotional memories.

6   By this I mean a metaphor emerges spontaneously and seems to capture the thoughts, mood or issue at hand and effectively orders our thought patterns.

7   These are metaphors used in everyday language, such as 'having one's head in the clouds'.

8   It is estimated (Johnson & Lakoff, 2003) that metaphor makes up some 75% of human language.

9   This is expanded on later with specific reference to Carl Jung's notion of the collective unconscious and the archetypes.

10 According Carl Jung (1969), psychic energy, once transformed through symbols, pops into consciousness as images/groups of images. This distinguishes them from physiological instincts. Archetypes organize these images – a process which is unconscious (before words or 'preverbal') and only palpable afterwards. This is when a dialogue between our ego (through the questions forming part of the animation process) is possible. This also elicits new symbols from the archetypal domain.

11 It is a form of thinking about one's thinking or speaking about speaking, based on gathering 'intelligence' or information (insight) about the contents or structure of one's thoughts or speech.

12 In *Metaphors We Live By*, Johnson and Lakoff (2003) refer to 'source domain' and 'target domain'. My emphasis is on 'donor' and 'recipient' as we really receive a gift from the 'giving' part of the metaphor. When we animate the metaphor in its positive guise, the meaning becomes clear.

13 These are merely triggers, which the nervous system imbues with meaning. Placed at the pinnacle of our minds, metaphor aids significantly our meaning making and changes.

14 Yet metaphors remain a sort of mental 'shorthand'. Work needs to be done to get beyond the words to the symbols and with that to their *meaning*.

Chapter 3

Metaphor Animation Works

If I could tell you what it meant, there would be no point in dancing it.
Isadora Duncan[1]

Make Your Metaphors Matter

The above quote suggests that symbolic representations (in this case, dance) contain a richer experiential base and communicative power that overcomes the constraints of words (and the conscious mind). By engaging with the attributes of the symbols, you are freed from the heavy limitations of words, including what the symbols themselves are called. This is important as words tie you to the past (past associations really), which if unfavorable can be an impediment to growth. The moment you put an experience into words, these experiences are overlaid with past memories, and thereby colored. In this way, the present is overshadowed by past associations. 'If a cow looks at an umbrella, it means nothing to it because an umbrella has no associations for a cow; for a human being it has dozens' (Wilson, 1983, p.37). Research[2] shows that in the case of visual sensory experience only a small fraction of 'information' (10–20%) comes from our retinas; the rest is imbued with pre-existing meaning from the mind itself (about 65%). It is this significantly bigger portion of mental 'baggage', which, as words, constrains us in terms of what we think we are capable of. Even if we think that we are capable of a lot, we can be capable of much more.

Words may not create thoughts per se, but play an important role in the manner in which the mind assimilates experiences and what associations are formed. Words tend to bias the mental processes into the direction of: (1) what is already known, with current experience being compared to memories of existing ones; (2) what we look for next. We will call this *actuality*, which obstructs the process of change and transformation (*potentiality*).

It was Albert Einstein who so poignantly spoke about the fact that 'the significant problems we face cannot be solved at the same level of thinking we were at when we created them'. Transformation through metaphor animation requires that we shift from actuality to *possibility*. With that we need to purge mere words and thereby past associations. How does the animation process achieve that?

- *First:* the animation process, by focusing on symbol attributes (what you hear, feel, see, smell, or taste) frees you from the constraints of words and past associations. It brings you back in touch with the pure sensory[3] infor-mation that first served as the building blocks of what you then termed or labeled, thereby creating some certainty but also imposing limitations on the richness of your experiential field. Metaphor animation is a renewed way of befriending your unconscious – the seat of lasting change – thereby creating a unified Self.
- *Second:* the unconscious mind 'trades' in a different currency – you need a 'currency translator' to reveal its content and transformative power to the conscious mind. This is *exactly* what the symbols do – they translate and convey the message in a manner that will avail the necessary resources for change to you and do so in a recognizable and understandable manner. Most impor-tantly, they will achieve this without you doing any form of interpretation. If we had to use a computer analogy, the symbols are like a program that is able to recognize a file extension (in this case, .COLUNS (dot.collective uncon-

scious)), thereby 'opening it' and revealing its contents.

- *Third:* the symbol animation process starts to help you explore and sketch a prospective (future) reality, free from words and limiting labels and driven by possibility. This facilitates a mental climate whereby the unconscious mind can generate its own meaning and scenarios, bringing forth resource symbols which eventually unlock the remedial, generative or transformative process you desired. This will translate into a strengthened sense of Self and ego.

- *Fourth:* the symbol animation process unlocks a creative process that is more three-dimensional and not constrained by the usual time-lines that dictate that the past is 'behind' and the future a 'headspace' somewhere 'up ahead'. It makes it possible to conceive a future 'reality' and live it now in the form of an 'as if' manifestation. Key to this process is that animation is driven by fantasy, creativity and intuition. This generates a whole metaphoric envelope, which in its animated form triggers the insight. It is when the whole picture falls into place that the breakthroughs happen. These breakthroughs can be humble and more remedial in nature, resulting in a widening mental headspace (generative), or fully transformative – which is experienced as renewal, like the wool has been pulled off your eyes and your perspectives are suddenly wider and deeper.

In order to animate the symbols as sub-components of metaphor – to unlock and decode their often hidden meaning, and imbue them with functions within the context of the metaphor as a whole, the questions set out in the next chapters work magic. Keep in mind as was explained in a previous chapter, that the building blocks of metaphor (symbols) are interrelated within the bounded metaphor envelope. When we start unpacking them, it will become evident what they mean:

- within the envelope (their function as metaphor building blocks and change resources for Self) (intra-relationships); and
- beyond it (others; beyond Self) (interrelationships; expectations of, and actions toward others).

The animation questions discussed later hinge on the principle discussed earlier (spider web analogy), namely that any changes in the sub-components (symbols) of the metaphor will affect the whole, either sustaining its current function or giving rise to new insights and meanings. These changes at the level of the symbols can be incremental (evolutionary or remedial, resulting in improved well-being: emotional state change) or revolutionary (transformation). When the symbol(s) or building block(s) on which the metaphor and its meaning hinges are enriched or altered, then the whole (metaphor) will be affected. This is much like identifying the load-bearing structures of a building – if these are interfered with, the whole building can come down. Working with non-'load bearing' elements, on the other hand, may bring about only cosmetic changes – a sort of mental 'facelift'. Working at the level of the whole (within and between metaphors) will inevitably bring about dramatic change or insight (evident as 'ordinary thoughts'), also at the level of the symbols (parts). It is important to remember that some symbols are merely supportive to making the whole and its meaning come about; others act as *resource symbols*, which alter the metaphor and with that its meaning and the insight it provides to the user (you). The minimum you can expect from this is that your metaphor envelope is explored in some detail and the symbols animated and that some relationships beyond the metaphor envelope are identified. Familiarizing yourself with the steps in the next chapters will teach you how to ripen the process further.

When going through the process in the next chapter, you may notice that by working with metaphor, insights or clarity may suddenly 'pop' into your mind as ordinary thoughts. This is an indication that the metaphor is being animated, which is necessary to discover which symbols are resources and do their change-work. Remember that since the metaphor mirrors your mind, the latter changes as the former does.

More on the Symbols' Role as Transformative Resources

METAPHORIC ENVELOPE	METAPHOR ANIMATION PROCESS (MAP): DECODING			
	Unpacking / Animating	Bursts of Insight	Unpacking / Animating	Change or Transformation (Whole)
METAPHORIC STREAM	• Entry			•
CONCEPTUAL STREAM				
SENSORY AND SUB-SENSORY STREAM (SYMBOLS)				Exit

Table 3.1: From metaphor to ordinary narrative: animation process

Metaphor decoding is the result of the metaphor animation process.

You would recall that the sensory and sub-sensory elements of the metaphor (its attributes) as you experience them through your 'mind's eye' consist of *what* they are and *how* they are experienced (sub-sensory: big or small; dim or clear; movement or still; loud or soft; textures, etc.[4]). This forms the basic building blocks of metaphor at the experiential level, qualifying it and introducing nuances, which enrich and provide greater clarity with impacts at an emotional level. Therefore, the objectives of the symbol-animating process include:

- discovering how you represent the metaphor and its

symbols to yourself. It is highly likely that there is much more to how the metaphor and its sub-sensory qualities represent themselves to your mind's eye. The refining and animating questions will assist in 'mining' the metaphor envelope and its symbols for more information.

- exploring the essential nature of the symbols with specific emphasis on creating conditions necessary for symbols to reveal their role as potential resources to:
  - you directly, as the 'beneficiary' of the metaphor; or
  - indirectly by impacting on other symbols[5] in the metaphor envelope, thereby unlocking the transformative or insight-generating function of, or progression in the metaphor.

The manifestations of symbols (as resources) as set out below can be distinguished. The animation process, by creating desirable conditions, seeks to lay bare the inherent resources of the symbols; their relationship to other symbols, the metaphor as a whole and to you as the metaphor-decoding 'beneficiary'. Often, the animation process reveals the explicit resources first. Symbols as resources should be viewed as processes (verbs) rather than things (nouns).

As explicit resources
Once you start animating the metaphor envelope, certain symbols will strike you right away as being resource symbols. You might think to yourself, 'This is important' or 'Wow'. Furthermore, their intention will be clear too! They are poised to get you out of the starting blocks and help you animate the envelope and provide directional force. These symbols can appear as mere objects, but there is often more to them than meets the eye. They appear to be layered, with meaning 'stacked' upon meaning, so always remain receptive to further insights being revealed.

As conditional resources

These symbols depend on other conditions in the metaphor envelope to be met; for other symbols to 'show their hand' or to express their desire. They are like the blossoms lying dormant in the seeds of a flower: they depend on the flower to grow (inherent condition) and for water and a nutrient-rich soil to be available (extrinsic conditions). Once the required conditions have been 'met', these symbols can reveal themselves and their intent or purpose quite unexpectedly. Here, animation is like tending a garden.

As dualistic resources

These symbols have a dual purpose, in that they prevent something from happening but in doing so also fulfill a security role. They sustain the current structure of the metaphor envelope and by implication the structure of your subjective experiential world. This is much like an airplane holding you 'captive' but at the same time keeping you safe and alive at high altitudes. These symbols will relinquish their role once the duality has been resolved, e.g. if the discomfort of staying 'put' (i.e. not enacting the directives of the metaphor) is outweighing the discomfort of rising to a challenge or fulfilling a dream.

As tacit resources

These symbols have much in store, but their function is not clear. You will have to apply meta-sensory techniques to work with the attributes ('how') of these symbols, determining if changing their size, location, etc. will make it clear what role they may fulfill. During the animation process which you will embark on soon, you have to pay attention to fine nuances, e.g. light bouncing off, or shimmering across the surface of the symbols.

As enigmatic resources

The purpose of enigmatic resource symbols *depends* on their function not being clear to the metaphor beneficiary. They are mysterious and will resist any attempts at revealing their purpose within the metaphor envelope. They may be like groundwater providing sustenance, without being visible to the beneficiary (plant, human or animal). They may fulfill the breakthrough function when the animation process 'arrives' at a threshold and starts to transform the metaphor envelope and with that, brings about the change desired.

As situational resources

As 'shape-shifters' or 'cyclers', these situational resources change their meaning/adopt a meaning depending on what is required at the given point in time. They are like a 'multi-tool' with many applications, depending on the context and situational requirements.

As redemptive resources

Being aimed at mental and emotional release from a past event(s), these symbols will make it possible to let go, thereby releasing the emotions or mental anguish related to these events. Consequently, more mental energy is available for a generative and prospective life orientation. Memories of past events that you want to let go of can be turned into a metaphor and then a RGT metaphor like any other issue. If you, for example, were to feel guilty about being nasty with someone, simply say: 'The guilt and regret I suffer because of being nasty with (person's name) is like...' This will evoke the negative metaphor. Then simply convert the negative metaphor into a positive metaphor by stating: 'Being free of all guilt and regret would be like...' After animating this RGT metaphor, you may feel unburdened. Alternatively, if you feel it necessary, you will have the strength to approach the person you feel you have wronged to say you are sorry or ask them for forgiveness. The animation process would have given you the clarity and ego-strength to resolve the matter.

As progress indicator resources
These are resource symbols that are different in name and in terms of their attributes but carry the same meaning, thus preventing progress. The animation process will make it clear that they are the same as the symbols already dealt with. The purpose of these symbols is to show that existing constraints or challenges are merely taking another guise. Therefore these symbols are useful as progress indicators (or if there is a lack thereof). These symbols won't appear if good progress is made.

As ripple-effect resources
Once these symbols reveal their purpose through animation, the insight they bring ripples through all the other symbols, imbuing the whole envelope with enlightenment. Suddenly everything fits into context and a coherent narrative unfolds.

Threshold or tipping-point resources
The symbols avail themselves only when the animation process has taken the RGT metaphor to the brink of transformation. They literally appear to provide the final nudge to bring about an epiphany that makes you realize that something dramatic is happening.

It is important to remember that resource symbols are catalysts for transformation. The animation process (resulting in decoding of the symbols/metaphor) reveals novel and/or additional properties. Resource symbols, however, also 'benefit' from a re-organization (causes and effects of change) of the whole metaphoric envelope (and commensurately changed meaning). They are the building blocks, but derive their meaning from the whole. Whilst the metaphor is still 'called' the same, its role and meaning would have changed for the metaphor animator (user) and (hopefully) brought about the desired transformation. As the figure below shows, the animation process is horizontal and evolutionary (continuous) and may provide bursts of insight as it progresses, resulting in resource symbols superseding 'ordinary' ('old' or 'pre-animation') symbols.

As the animation process results in the maturation of the metaphoric envelope and its symbols, threshold/edge conditions should be reached. A fundamental break with the understanding and meaning of the pre-animation RGT metaphor takes place and new meanings arise. One can think about this as a form of inundation, like a sponge that can absorb no more liquid. Just think about sitting in a traffic jam. You may notice that there are many different cars around you, from small and cheap ones to the very grand and extremely fast ones. The traffic jam levels the playing field among these cars and their drivers, in spite of their differences. The cheapest and slowest car is effectively on par with the most expensive, fast and luxurious. Speed won't help in a traffic jam and although comfort and an air-conditioner may make the situation more bearable, none of these factors will get you out of the jam and where you want to be. Within the context of the latter, all options have come to a point of inundation, and the commuters walking or riding a motorbike or bicycle will make the most progress. These simplest of characteristics (narrowness and maneuverability of the two-wheelers) have the upper hand. The animation process helps create a situation whereby all options are explored and brought to a point of saturation and complexity. Ultimately, this leads to the emergence of a simple but illuminating solution (like the 'bicycle'), revealed by the resource symbols. This simplicity will strike you instantaneously, so be alert so as not to miss it. It is discontinuous (sudden and unexpected), like a deep and vast canyon arising in a flat landscape, creating a break with the past (the process thus far), drawing attention to a new reality (and requiring other resources). If the conditions are 'ripe' only a small nudge is required to bring about the change in meaning and renewed understanding which is tantamount to 'hitting a mental or attitudinal reset button'. This brings simplicity to the metaphor envelope and with that, simplicity and relief in terms of 'ordinary thoughts' about one's life and issues. The unconscious mind would have achieved most of the tasks of fostering the insight – the additional nudge may come when the conscious mind becomes aware of the change and helps mold it.

Remember: if the conditions are right a butterfly flapping its wings in New York can result in a tropical storm in the Caribbean (Capra, 1997).

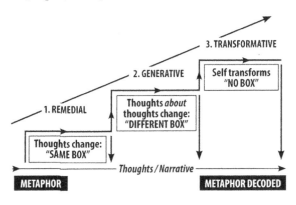

Figure 3.1: Remedial, Generative and Transformative impacts explained

The above reflects three tiers of change: If you were a house, 'remedial' would mean that you make alterations and additions. 'Generative' would mean that you start questioning why the thought of renovations actually exists and what purpose it has. You may tear down the house and build a new one. 'Transformative' means that you redefine yourself and your purpose (e.g. becoming a nomad), possibly obviating the need for a house, irrespective of old or new. The increasing gradient in the diagram above shows change yielded by animation (which is horizontal); the downward arrows influence: (1) how we think; (2) how we think about thinking (why we have certain thoughts/questions); and (3) who we are (discontinuous – revolutionary – holistic).

To explain a little further: I prefer to think about the three-level process below as being like the 'cat eyes' embedded in asphalt road surfaces. They only glow to show you the way or keep you on the road when your car's lights shine on them. Once you have passed by, they drop back into the darkness. This is like change at levels 1 and 2, which still involves the conscious mind to a large extent even though the symbols bring about deeper self-awareness and insight. Some effort goes into sustaining the conscious change. Level 3 transformation on the other hand is facilitated 95% by the collective unconscious and the archetypes. It is the type of 'cat eye' often seen on temporary roads or detours that already has a glow inside (battery powered), like hot ambers covered by a layer of ash. Lights don't need to shine on it. The conscious mind merely has to focus the light and harness its meaning, like blowing on the coals to remove the ashes, make them glow brilliantly and put them to use. The ego is like the 'passive' cat eyes – it exists largely due to an outside light source (contact with and inputs from the world). The unconscious is like the 'active' cat eyes – it has a glow inside even if there's no input from the outside world. It will show you the way and keep you on the road and lead you to your destination from the inside-out. This is authentic and enduring transformation.

The above can be summarized as followed:

i. Level 1: Remedial ('What'): (*you get answers to your existing questions that satisfy you*): Your thoughts and emotions change (primary level), providing brief and situational relief, dealing with an issue on a piecemeal basis. Behavioral change at this level will follow. On the scale of impact, remedial is 'third prize'.

ii. Level 2: Generative ('Why') (*you realize that you have been asking the wrong/self-limiting questions*): Your thoughts about your thoughts (the 'meta-methods' or programs which you invoke to think about life and yourself, rather than just the thoughts themselves) change. One can think of this as *self-reflections about how you reflect* about your life or yourself. An example would be to inspect and alter the expectations you have about the world/yourself and which may have led to discontentment when things don't work out as expected. You would question why you had certain questions/expectations in the first place. Why is this important? For learning to take place, your mind needs to have (new) questions, otherwise it knows only what it sees and sees only what it knows. For example, you may have asked yourself why you aren't as rich as your neighbor. The answers to that question may be varied, but are unlikely to be satisfactory. Furthermore, you may ask yourself that same question as you get richer ('Why am I not even richer; richer than the neighbor down the road?'). If you start changing the question (which the decoding process will facilitate), you may focus on what you already have, rather than what you are missing. This would result in a new question: 'Why don't I just focus on what I have and be content?' This will certainly reduce angst about missing (and needing to pursue) ever higher levels of riches. (As research has shown, people readily adjust their lifestyle to get on par with the increasing amount of money they make. This shows why a question: 'Why am I not rich?' never really gets answered in a definitive manner.) New questions (curiosity, really) on the other hand will make you reach into the world and look for new information.

This will result in new beliefs[6] emerging. The changed beliefs and alternative expectations at this level will result in novel behavior. The new beliefs that arise, in turn, have to be inspected again. This level is all about greater awareness about *how/why* we know *that* we know things about our reality and also *what* things we know about our reality On the scale of impact, generative is 'second prize'.

iii. Level 3: Transformative ('Who') (*you change*): the person who has the thoughts (secondary) about the thoughts (primary) changes (often very suddenly). Change happens at a holistic level and not piecemeal as is the case under levels 1 and 2. This is figuratively 'hitting the mental re-set button' – resulting in a forward-looking, clean 'mental slate'. You have simply outgrown a previous state. This is akin to changing from a turntable (analog: to listen to vinyl records) to switching to CDs (digital). As mental 'edge' processes, they result in simplification when complexity no longer yields fruits – a new order arises and change resonates at the level of your Self. Typically this involves changes at the level of the very root of who you are. Often, this sort of dramatic change takes a truly life-altering event(s) – often thrust upon us without choice. Some people who have had near-death experiences, for example, have subsequently changed fundamentally – at the very core of their being, with the change resonating in every cell of their body. Luckily, by working with RGT metaphor, the same transformation can be achieved, provided that the process is worked through diligently, patiently and with an open mind.

Over time, new questions will arise about the 'changed you' that require answers, simply because growth is never definitive and new challenges arise.

Behavior will respond to the new orientation of Self. The systems theory guru, Gregory Batson, talked about 'the difference that makes the difference'. Perhaps he meant that you recognize the change or distance between where you were and where you are now as being fundamentally significant. It does not have to be a big difference that 'makes the difference' – it is whether it matters to you and is recognized as such at some level of your *Self*. On the scale of impact, transformative is 'first prize'.

As the hierarchy below shows, upward change is possible but usually incremental, yielding insights and change on a piecemeal basis. Downward transformation is brought about by (and indeed requires) an epiphany. Change happens at the level of the 'whole', rather than at the level of your thoughts ('what') and beliefs ('why'). These all change commensurate with insight into the transformative/generative/remedial metaphor. The most important thing to remember is that the overarching will always change the underlying. If, through the symbol animation process, your questions start to change, the answers will change too. What you are now getting by way of answers may surprise you as they don't relate to what your initial questions were!

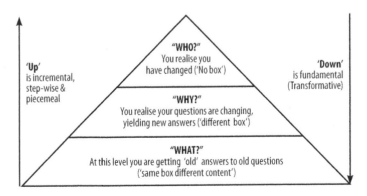

Figure 3.2: Step-wise vs. fundamental/discontinuous change

They have ceased to be important, as they are *old answers to old questions*. The new questions will put you on a path to insight.

Summary

✓ By engaging with the sense-based attributes of the symbols (which is what animation does), you are freed from the constraints of words, including what the symbols themselves are called. Symbols contain a richer experiential base and communicative power and supersede the constraints of words. Words tend to direct mental processes toward what is already known (actuality), rather than what could be (*potentiality*). (The next chapters will show you exactly how).

✓ By engaging with the symbols you take the metaphor as a whole to tipping-point conditions, where fundamental change can occur. You then experience this change subjectively. These changes at the level of the symbols can be incremental, resulting in increased well-being or freedom from symptoms, or revolutionary (total transformation). When the symbol(s) or building block(s) on which the metaphor and its meaning hinges are enriched or altered, then the whole will be affected too.

✓ Animating symbols contained in the metaphor envelope helps you translate and convey unconscious remedial, generative or transformative messages in a manner that creates insight. Symbols are the 'currency converters' needed to make the unconscious resources conscious. However, conscious interpretation is neither required nor desirable. Your conscious mind simply holds the door ajar to let the messenger (symbols) and message (their meaning) in.

✓ Symbol animation unlocks possibility and what becomes known will strengthen your ego without inflating it and will restore your Self as the center of your being. As your ego (the conscious center of your psyche) assimilates contents from your unconscious via the symbols in the RGT metaphor envelope, it is progressively more balanced against the Self, resulting in blissful wholeness within you. 'From the standpoint of the Self, the ego is a working hypothesis. The ego has no substantive reality, but is an *enabling fiction* that allows something greater to express itself.'[7]

✓ Symbol animation unlocks a three-dimensional creative visualization process not constrained by the usual time-lines that dictate that the past is 'behind' and the future a 'headspace' (or place) somewhere 'up ahead'. It creates a history of the future, pulling it toward the here and now.

✓ The fundamental project of metaphor animation is to explore the symbols, how they present themselves to you, and what transformative payload they carry for you as the metaphor beneficiary. There are various symbols, some of which are explicit (you know their function immediately) whereas others are more tacit; with some even resisting animation. These are often symbols that are ambivalent or dualistic – they protect you but also prevent you from attaining the desired change. The animation process will, however, finally make the symbols reveal their meaning when the necessary conditions have been met.

✓ Metaphor animation is experiential. If metaphor is indeed grounded in the body as Feldman (2006) suggests, animating metaphor will impact the body and emotions, which arise there.

✓ Insights that strike you quite suddenly are an indicator that the animation process is bearing fruits. (As the metaphor is enriched, so are you, as you are actively attending to your own mind and brain – the latter changes structurally through neural plasticity.[8)]

✓ The fruits of RGT metaphor animation take the form of a

continuum:

○ *remedial change (change in thinking),* which involves getting new and unexpected answers to your existing questions. The results are impressive but limited in scope.

○ *generative change (change in thinking about thinking)*: the programs or filters (expectations) *that you use to make sense of your own thoughts* and the world around you change, rather than just your thoughts (reflection about reflection). Think of this as new questions arising rather than answers emerging to existing questions. New questions point you to new information. Your thoughts about your thoughts change. This results in a generative boost to propel you forward. You are now 'out of the box'.

○ *transformative change (change in the person having the thoughts)*: you change, and your existing beliefs are renewed holistically. This is like hitting the figurative mental 're-set button'. The change is not incremental but fundamental. You will experience a distinct discontinuity between how you first experienced your world and yourself and how you are now.

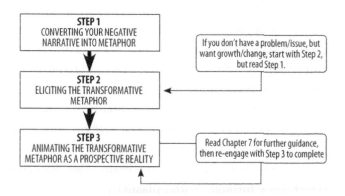

Figure 3.3: Metaphor animation road-map

Armed with this background knowledge, let's embark on the journey of decoding our metaphor and with that, impact heavily on our experiences, thoughts and behavior – for the better.

Above is a road-map of the metaphor animation process you will embark on in the next chapter:

ENDNOTES

1   Bateson, 1972, p.137.

2   Gregory, 1999.

3   This sensory input does not come from the outside world but from the unconscious – a picture from within.

4   Refer to Chapter 2 for further information on the sub-sensory qualities that the symbols can present with.

5   Some of the symbols in the envelope may be 'unwilling' to move, because they fulfill a protective function(s) or because the conditions necessary for them to 'step into the fold' have not yet been met.

6   Beliefs are here defined as what we actively construct in our minds about our 'reality' and then hold to be true. Beliefs aren't objective but our validated thoughts that we believe to be true and often hold onto obstinately. This is probably because of our significant emotional investment in and maintenance thereof, but to the active exclusion of competing (and possibly unsettling) 'information'.

7   Tacey, 2006, p.45.

8   What we were 'given' as our brain was always thought to be 'it' with no prospect of expanding this precious resource. Those 1970s and 1980s theories are luckily out of the window. The brain is literally 'plastic'. It can grow and remain supple like any muscle. Lost functions can be recovered by those areas that are still intact. However, we have to engage our brains and make them our best friends. They seem to understand the language of metaphor and metaphor animation as a mode of change particularly well.

Chapter 4

Step 1: Converting Negative Narrative into Metaphor

Narrative No More

By converting everyday negative narrative into metaphor you are embarking on a journey of insight and transformation that cannot be easily obtained through mere words and ordinary thought patterns. By eliciting metaphor you are assisting your unconscious mind to shape and pre-package information into a form which will facilitate your animation process. This will put you on the path of critical insights necessary to attain the change that you have always yearned for, but had difficulty obtaining, given the constraints imposed by the sheer volume of thoughts and associated emotions. If claims that we have tens of thousands of thoughts per day[1] are true, then it becomes immediately evident that the coherence offered by metaphors is critically necessary. It enables us to make better sense of our thoughts about Self, others, relationships and life. In fact, the shortcoming which many self-help books and therapies have in common is that they rely on words. Using words overwhelms thoughts that are already in disarray with yet more information, which has to be processed and applied. More emotional confusion and yet more mental anguish can result. This is like fighting fire with fire (which occasionally works, such as when burning oil wells are robbed of oxygen through detonations, thus snuffing out the flames). Mostly though, more elegant solutions are required such as those offered by metaphor decoding for personal transformation and growth.

With that introduction, I now invite you to think of any issue or something (X, Y or Z) that you are not happy with at the moment. This issue may arise spontaneously as a metaphor or a day-to-day narrative (non-metaphoric description). If the issue spontaneously arises in the form of a metaphor, go to Step 2 (in the next chapter). If the issue is 'stuck' at the level of words or body-language,[2] ask the following simple but highly effective metaphor eliciting question:

MAIN TASK
'What is X, Y or Z *LIKE*?'
WRITE THIS DOWN NOW ON A BIG PIECE OF PAPER
FOR LATER REFERENCE.

It is critical to let the metaphor arise spontaneously and intuitively, and to go with whatever comes up first. The idea is not to let the conscious mind edit the metaphor or to take a critical view on it and try to come up with something 'smarter'[3] or even more appropriate. The unconscious mind has the answers, so it is better to let it rule the roost. Remember, there are no wrong answers.

What happens here is that you start 'meta-communicating' (to yourself or others) about your life issue or challenge – you *communicate about communicating*, or *make a statement about a statement* by re-articulating ordinary narrative in the form of 'like', thus rising above it. This is like looking at a valley after arriving at the top of a mountain, rather than being stuck on the rock-face. Being on top of the mountain or looking from afar in the valley provides a perspective, which allows for an evaluation of the route taken through the valley and up the mountain. The clarity from these positions would be vast and panoramic, allowing for certain problems or route alternatives to be identified. This allows one to enjoy the view en route too, as opposed to slogging away at the obstacles before one.

'Negative Metaphor'

Strictly speaking, a metaphor is never negative per se. It may merely be conveying something you experience as negative. If you start with a problem or issue and ask, 'What is it LIKE?', a 'negative' metaphor is likely to emerge. This would be a necessary first step only if you are experiencing something negative or problematic that you want to change. If you start with a wish or a positive point of departure, you can move directly to Step 2, but ensure you read about Step 1 for further clarity.

How the Word 'Like' Elicits the Metaphor

Whilst it is not a requirement for metaphor to be identified by 'like', using the word in a clarifying sentence seems to result in the spontaneous elicitation of metaphor. Many metaphors include the word 'like', e.g. 'The idea struck me *like* a bolt out of the blue.' In other instances, the donor notion is simply equated to the recipient term, as in 'Life *is* a song' ['life' (recipient term) is a 'song' (donor notion)]. In the poetic sphere, the word 'like' often forms part of a metaphoric expression, but 'like' is not a requirement to phrase a metaphor. The transformative power of metaphor is as awesome as its communicative impact. This will be immediately clear to anyone who has been deeply moved by metaphor at an emotional and cognitive level, when watching a movie or reading something laden with metaphor.

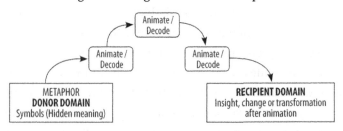

Figure 4.1: Decoding process: insight revealed and transferred to recipient domain

Example:

Recently, I asked someone during a coaching session: 'How are things?' The person responded: 'My life is aimlessly wandering.' By doing so, they had already captured their dilemma in the form of a metaphor, the donor domain 'aimlessly wandering', potentially alluding to a journey without direction, with this being superimposed on the recipient domain ('life'). If they hadn't generated a metaphor, my question, 'How are things?' could have resulted in a response such as, 'I'm not sure' or 'It is not going well'. Then the question, 'What is "It is not going well" *like*?' would have elicited a metaphor such as the one volunteered up-front.

What does the elicitation of metaphor (whether generative, remedial or transformative) do? It fulfills the following important functions:

i.   It captures the dilemma at hand ('It is like...') with some accuracy, making it less confusing and easier to attend to. It therefore taps less into mental resources than a mere string of words that seek to express a problem or need for change. It removes confusing mental clutter, leaving only the gems that can be more easily mined. It is better to generate separate metaphors for all issues and questions than to attend to the thought patterns reflecting them.

ii. It provides a fairly strong hint as to what domain or aspect is problematic or requires transformation. This creates a focus area, which can be dealt with more easily. Such focus areas can include Self, others, relationships, etc. Furthermore, raw material needed for the transformative metaphor (see Step 2, next chapter) to be unbundled is provided.

Metaphors, however, don't need to refer to a personal, work or life challenge (remedial purpose of metaphor), but can also denote something positive, an aspiration or something you may want more of (generative purpose of metaphor). If you find that you want *more of something positive*, rather than *less of something negative*, start with a WISH. For example, 'I wish I were more kind to my partner.' Then, evoke an R (remedial), G (generative) or T (transformative) metaphor through the following simple question: 'Kind to my partner like what?' This should yield a metaphor such as 'Kind to my partner like a gentle summer breeze.' You then work with this metaphor as it is richer and higher up (see table below), rather than with the more fuzzy, non-descript and unbounded notion of 'more kind to my partner'.The 'donor domain' contains symbols (overt and covert)

RECIPIENT DOMAIN (PRE-METAPHOR)	DONOR DOMAIN (TO BE ANIMATED)
	"…like a gentle summer breeze".
"…kind to my partner.…"	

Table 4.1: Clarification of donor and recipient domains

which are yet to be discovered and animated. Once this has been done, the 'gift' is donated to the recipient domain, benefiting you as the metaphor beneficiary. That which appears as mere words in the donor domain ('gentle summer breeze') are actually symbols or symbol precursors. The latter are therefore the contents of the RGT metaphor prior to the animation process starting. They create the receptacles to 'receive' the actual symbols (or additional symbols where symbols already exist in the donor domain) to make them proliferate. You could think about this as creating a little garden with rich and fertile soil that is poised to receive seeds, which in turn become plants. Through love and care, you make the seeds come to fruition and make the plants thrive.

Summary

- ✓ By converting everyday thoughts about an expectation, dream or problem into metaphor, you *stop thinking* about the related underlying thoughts and *start thinking* in terms of the metaphor that availed itself.
- ✓ Immediately, overwhelming mental clutter is removed and the *donor domain/notions*, which enlighten the *recipient domain*, are available to you. The donor domain signifies something about the issue you intend working with. This is the first crucial step to start making sense and growing.
- ✓ That which appears as mere words in the metaphor is symbols (unconscious resources) or the basis for further symbols to be evoked and enriched during the process of animation.
- ✓ The approaches set out in the next chapter are about converting the negative or non-generative metaphor into a remedial, generative and transformative metaphor.

ENDNOTES

1   And these are only the ones we become aware of. Due to selective attention, many thoughts and feelings never come to the attention of the conscious mind and simply pass us by.

2   Not only language lends itself to conversion into metaphor. This works for posture changes, gestures, pointing by using the body, sighs, throat clearing, eye movements, etc.

3   Your own ego may be tempted to go to work on 'analyzing' the metaphor as it (typically) thinks it knows all the answers. However, as this and the next steps will show, the unconscious mind has a few rather awesome 'tricks up its sleeve'. So try to resist the urge to take the metaphor to task without the aid of this text.

Chapter 5

Step 2: Eliciting the Transformative (RGT) Metaphor

Often when people are facing a challenge, they spontaneously generate a metaphor that captures it. These can be impressions relating to current, future or past events which may keep them stuck or laboring under guilt or shame. This book seeks to focus on the generative and non-therapeutic/clinical application of metaphor. Therefore, conversion of the issue at hand (reflected through a negative metaphor), into a positive one - is the second step. The reasons are simple: metaphor is a remedial, generative or transformative resource. We seek to use the RGT metaphor as a facilitative, outcome - and direction-setting resource, thus creating a point of departure whereby thought patterns and emotions are directed by an intent of 'moving towards something positive', rather than 'away from something negative'. In so doing, other mental and emotional resources are mobilized and brought to bear on the issue or aspiration at hand; fear or anxiety becomes hope and anticipation – our attitudes change. Generating the positive, transformative metaphor and locating it in the bounded metaphor envelope ensures that the process of eliciting new unconscious symbols and their novel associations needed for change, remains constructive. Had we stayed with the 'negative' metaphor, we would have run the risk of being stuck in an unproductive cycle of existing negative associations when introspectively engaging with our unconscious mind. Vitality and renewal would have remained elusive.

Once the generative metaphor is elicited, the old (negative) metaphor ceases to exist and is superseded by the new one. A colloquial quantum leap takes place as the new and generative metaphor usually arises spontaneously without going through any intermittent, formative stages. If this does happen it occurs way before we are consciously aware of it. It does not arise in parts or by various alternative metaphors being 'tried on for size'. It is revolutionary rather than evolutionary. It is immediately suitable and entirely coherent as a whole, which is necessary for the meaning to be evident for the metaphor user. However, since it is born out of the negative metaphor, some of the parts of the old metaphor are retained, but only implicitly, to aid in the emergence of a generative metaphor and the animation thereof (more on this later). (Think of this as a tree that grows and thrives, with its previous stages of development 'smeared' all over its roots, branches and leafs, echoing its past). It captures these elements, which were previously part of a coherent but negative metaphor and shapes them in a hierarchical fashion. The downward arrow next to the pyramid in the figure below indicates that the metaphor as a whole contains the meaning (dominant). It is notably the donor information which dictates what is happening at the conceptual and sensory building block level, but not vice versa. The lower levels are defined by the overarching meaning, which only exists as a whole. The parts themselves in isolation would convey very little useful information. However, the lower levels are necessary building blocks, without which the metaphor will break down in its entirety.

Unlike the mountain analogy used in the previous chapter, positive metaphor allows you to do a 'virtual climb' up the mountain of life, identify the best route, and then go back and do the actual climb, sailing through an otherwise complex and emotionally taxing environment. In other words, it is not necessary to struggle up dead ends or difficult routes (even if some perceive these to be 'character building') – only to learn from mistakes after the fact – the typical 'hindsight with 20/20 vision' scenario.

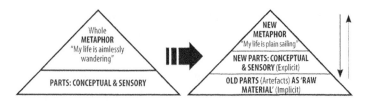

Figure 5.1: From old (negative) to RGT (positive) metaphor

The parts of the 'negative' metaphor (the whole ceases to exist) are retained, however, to be 'mined' for raw material. This process is usually unconscious. The negative metaphor, as you would recall, helps define what aspect (e.g. Self, relationships with others) has to be dealt with. It is interesting to note that the positive or generative metaphor is thematically similar to the negative metaphor. For example, the above pyramids show that both contain elements of journeys ('aimlessly wandering' and 'plain sailing').

The generative metaphor is all that the old one was *not*. The old parts as raw material ensure that this is achieved. If we compare the old (non-generative metaphor) with the new one, this becomes evident.

Exercise to Elicit the Transformative Metaphor

Turning a negative metaphor into a positive and generative one, takes one simple question:

MAIN TASK: ASK YOURSELF THE FOLLOWING QUESTION:
NOW, if my [INSERT WISH/DREAM/ASPIRATION HERE] were exactly as I want it to be, it would be LIKE...
WRITE THIS DOWN ON A LARGE PIECE OF PAPER.

Step-wise progression toward the RGT metaphor

Sometimes, however, the elicitation of the RGT metaphor is a step-wise process, i.e. that you begin with a metaphor *precursor* (different from symbol precursors). If, for example, you were to feel that you need to 'pull yourself together', this already is halfway to a metaphor, but it doesn't tell you LIKE WHAT. Thus, the donor domain is missing. You would still have to ask: 'Pull myself together *like what?*' This may yield, 'Pull myself together like a blanket on a cold winter night.'

The RGT metaphor as a gesture

The RGT metaphor can also start with a gesture. You have to learn to self-monitor your gestures to pick up on this. It is easiest to pick up on gestures by monitoring what others do. For example, if you ask someone about their life, they might waggle their hand from side to side in an indecisive manner – 'My life is [waggles hand].' If they were to translate the 'waggle' as per the task below, they would come up with the RGT metaphor. You may have also seen someone say, 'I have had it up to here [places hand under nose].' In response to the eliciting question below, this would perhaps elicit a metaphor about drowning in some sort of trouble or being fed up with something.

MAIN TASK FOR A GESTURE: ASK YOURSELF THE FOLLOWING QUESTION:
NOW, if my [INSERT WISH/DREAM/ASPIRATION HERE] were exactly as I want it to be, it would be LIKE [VERBALIZE YOUR GESTURE] WRITE THIS DOWN ON A LARGE PIECE OF PAPER.

The RGT metaphor as a sound effect

You may also find that you make a sound effect instead of verbalizing the metaphor outright. Perhaps it is true that men do this more often, e.g. instead of stating, 'If my relationship with my wife were everything I wanted it to be, it would be a jet flying by', the phrase 'a jet flying by' might be replaced by *'swooooosh'* (to denote the sound of a jet).

The task for the sound effect below is slightly different because it is difficult to make a sound effect and say what it is at the same time.

MAIN TASK FOR A SOUND EFFECT: ASK YOURSELF THE FOLLOWING QUESTION:
NOW, if my [INSERT WISH/DREAM/ASPIRATION HERE] were exactly as I want it to be, it would be [INSERT SOUND EFFECT HERE], which is LIKE [INSERT YOUR RGT METAPHOR HERE]
WRITE THIS DOWN ON A LARGE PIECE OF PAPER.

The RGT metaphor as bodily sensation

The RGT metaphor could also emerge as a bodily sensation. For example, in response to the question, 'If my emotional states were everything I wanted it to be, it would be like...' you might get a bodily sensation, e.g. gooseflesh running up and down your body. Alternatively, you might become aware of a gut-feel that is as yet unclear.

MAIN TASK FOR A BODILY SENSATION: ASK YOURSELF THE FOLLOWING QUESTION:
NOW, if my [INSERT WISH/DREAM/ASPIRATION HERE] were exactly as I want it to be, it would be like [PUT INTO WORDS THE BODILY SENSATION THAT YOU FEEL AND WHERE IT OCCURS].
WRITE THIS DOWN ON A LARGE PIECE OF PAPER.

Putting the sensation into words (verbalizing) clarifies it. If you had stated, 'If my emotional state were everything I wanted it to be, it would be like butterflies in my stomach', you would have labeled the initial flurry in your stomach. The 'butterflies in your stomach' would be the donor domain clarifying what is seen to be the emotion (recipient domain) that you desire. You would work toward this scenario of having 'butterflies in your stomach' by animating the RGT metaphor.

Irrespective of the source of the RGT metaphor, something really quite magical (in the true style of metaphors) happens immediately: A positive metaphor emerges spontaneously and effortlessly, which contains all the raw facilitative and direction-setting material required to achieve the positive change or transformation sought. The generative metaphor becomes the new point of departure. It reflects your wishes and desires! Being 'top of mind', this positive metaphor becomes a 'meta-cognitive driver' or attractor, directing other thought patterns toward achieving a certain outcome as concretized in the metaphor. It does so because the metaphor was generated by the unconscious mind, with little or no participation by the conscious mind. The unconscious mind seems totally adept at generating metaphor perfectly. Libet[1] found that everything we eventually become conscious of (as pictures, sounds or words) is generated some 500ms (milliseconds) (half a second) prior. That we become aware of things at the very instance that they happen is therefore an illusion. Our brain simply backdates conscious perceptions to create the impression that we are in synch with the external world or that our thoughts become conscious as they are 'created'. Actually we are half a second out of synch with ourselves. In this time, the unconscious mind is able to generate the RGT metaphor and constellate symbols which we then become consciously aware of. The positive metaphor (like the negative metaphor preceding it) can be taken to have been validated – a 'green light' by the unconscious, giving the 'go-ahead' and illuminating the way forward.

Example:

Taking the earlier example further, you would recall that the person had depicted their dilemma as 'My life is aimlessly wandering', thereby clarifying the aspect or domain ('life') that they felt was not working out well. I put the following question to the person: 'NOW, if your life were exactly as you want it to be, it would be LIKE...' The following was the response: 'My life would be (like) plain sailing' (generative metaphor).

For the moment, the RGT metaphor is static from the perspective of facilitating insight, change, or transformation. It is therefore critical to turn static metaphor sub-components or symbols into an animated state – to give them the 'kiss of life'. Therefore, you need to see the metaphor sub-components as symbols which have a function or act as resources to help you attain your outcome. If we see symbols in this light, it becomes apparent that they don't stand for something else (the common understanding, e.g. the cross as a symbol of faith). Rather, symbols (being contained in the donor domain) are an active function of the unconscious mind[2] – catalysts that provide perspective, renewal, vitality, or redemption way in excess of what the conscious 'I' (or ego) is capable of with its limited vista and resources. They are particularly useful to resolve psychological gridlocks or seemingly irreconcilable positions or wants.

It is critical to remember that by creating a positive (RGT) metaphor, the unconscious creates an envelope or holding environment as well as a workspace to do its change-work, 'using' resource symbols. Imbuing the envelope with seeds of change, it creates the roots for a fertile imagination – a requirement to achieve what the positive metaphor holds as a promise and potentiality. Also, by laying the foundations, a bond is created between the unconscious and the envelope, securing its commitment to 'build the house', which is the fully animated metaphor that can bring about the change that you desire.

I'll expand a little more on this in later chapters. For the purpose of this chapter it is important to remember that the positive metaphor is the envelope for symbol formation and animation, a safe and contained vessel for change, much like a cocoon is for a caterpillar poised to turn into a butterfly.

Remember: your ego exists *because* of its contact, through the masks you wear, with the outside world and can be inflated by it; the Self exists in *spite of it*.

The whole project of metaphor animation is to rebalance the situation whereby (quoting George Carlin), "the caterpillar does all the work and the butterfly gets all the glory". (Think of the caterpillar as the unconscious mind, the ego as the butterfly).

Summary

✓ This chapter would have allowed you to free yourself from the shackles of *actuality* (the negatively stated metaphor) and start the journey toward *possibility* (positively stated metaphor). The RGT metaphor envelope is the context for the animation process which harnesses possibility and makes it manifest in your life.

✓ The RGT metaphor animation process lets you 'dance it'. It is so rich that you wouldn't be able to say it. As I will remind you later, you need to draw and color-in your emerging RGT metaphor with all its symbols and how they are related to make up a coherent whole. This will become the picture containing the new associations, availed by the unconscious to facilitate the change you pursue.

✓ The RGT metaphor contains all the raw facilitative and direction-setting resources to achieve what is contained in it (your outcome).

✓ Being top of mind (a representation of a representation – the latter being of your experience captured as your ordinary thoughts), the RGT channels your thoughts toward the outcome(s) you desire. It does so by harnessing unconscious energy in the form of symbols.

✓ The RGT metaphor is perfectly and definitively created by the unconscious way before the conscious mind becomes aware of it. The conscious mind can add little by way of value – it merely stands in the service of the metaphor and the animation process.

✓ The contents of the negative metaphor (see Chapter 4) would have informed the RGT metaphor, as they tend to be thematically similar. In other words, aspects of the negative metaphor resonate in the RGT metaphor.

✓ By creating a RGT metaphor, the unconscious mind creates for itself a workspace for change-work, facilitated by the animation process, which brings forth the resource symbols. By creating this envelope, the unconscious mind forms a bond with the envelope and also commits itself to yielding the resource symbols.

✓ The envelope serves as a safe and bounded 'holding environment' in which change can be explored, attained and tested.

For the next chapter, ensure that:

• you have written down your positive RGT metaphor based on this chapter and the tasks set out in it;

• you have a large piece of paper and color pens/pencils, crayons, brushes and watercolors available. This is when the fun starts.

ENDNOTES

1   Carter, 2002.
2   Jung, 1959.

Chapter 6

Step 3: Animating the RGT Metaphor as a Future Reality

You rise and fall like water
You try to stay the same
The only thing that's certain
is that everything will change.
Bob Seger, The Answer's in the Question

The Transformative Metaphor as Your New Reality

It is absolutely critical for you to approach the symbol-animating process (see forthcoming questions) with the following:

- *the mindset that you have already attained the outcome encoded in the metaphor;* and
- *pretend*[1] *that you know its meaning and the role of its symbols.*

You will observe that the above mindset makes a huge difference in how the symbols in the metaphor envelope emerge and how illuminated, visceral and personalized the metaphor experience becomes. This accelerates the process of unpacking the transformative nature of metaphor and its symbols and the achievement of the desired outcome. Furthermore, you are starting to tap into the vast resources of visualization (driven by curiosity), moving from the actual (current reality) to the prospective (future possibility). Knowing about your destination or journey is necessary to help you align your mental resources with a *prospective reality as if that reality already existed.*

The mental picture of that reality in fact already exists and is tacitly reflected in the metaphor about the desired outcome (process and result elements). According to Einstein, 'the distinction between past, present and future is only a stubbornly persistent illusion'. The mind is therefore quite willing to accept an 'as if' scenario (visualized reality) in quite the same way as it would deal with 'real' inputs through the senses. Actually, the animation and decoding process is all about rehearsing scenarios. As is the case with any exercise: if you do it repetitively, it becomes second nature. This is why sports people go through the motions in their mind's eye, before they have even arrived at the sports field. They then re-enact their mental reality, by superimposing it on the 'real' reality.

The unconscious mind with its awesome information-processing ability[2] is completely capable of doing this 'time-travel'. It thereby transcends all current constraints and articulates a future scenario that you can work towards using the other steps below. One can think of this as a form of *remembered future*, whereby all you have experienced in the past is transformed and this actuality becomes future possibility manifesting right now. This is a form of apperception, as the newly observed associations attached to the emerging metaphor symbols are related to past experience which spans the personal and notably the collective unconscious (which transcends the individual psyche). Using the RGT metaphor as a bounded envelope is safe as it constitutes a *Probierbühne* (rehearsal stage) with an audience (source of the ego's projected preoccupation with competitiveness, failure and embarrassment) not being present. Resources simply have to be applied to make the leap from where/who you are to where/who you want to be.

After all, when we want something we need to know how it is when we 'arrive'. Otherwise we would have attained that highly desirable point without actually recognizing it and simply pass it by, like missing an unlit destination in the dead of night. RGT metaphor gives us a sense of that place.

NOW, take the following animating questions to your generative metaphor, as if it were already real and in the *here and now*.

The Animating Questions:[3] Attaining the RGT Metaphor Outcomes

After the background below, the metaphor animation questions appear for you to apply.

Background

Some 80% of what we experience is visual and out of the estimated 100 billion neurons a vast number is dedicated to 'processing' visual information. Consequently, the attributes of the symbols of metaphors are also often visual in nature (images), at least on the surface. As you animate your RGT metaphor you may become aware, however, that they often involve all the senses, but most notably also hearing and touch.

Although the generative metaphor contains all the resources that you will require to achieve deep and lasting change, it may appear quite one-dimensional and static, belying the resources locked up within it. This is why an animation process is necessary.

The first step in the animation process is to write down the RGT metaphor, as per the instruction in Chapter 5. It is important that you mentally 'freeze' or bracket the metaphor to stay focused and to prevent other (including negative) metaphors about other issues or their symbols popping into your mind and blurring your attention.

For illustrative and clarification purposes I am going to continue with the 'plain sailing' example: *'My life is (like) plain sailing.'* In its current format, the metaphor reveals very little; apparently only a potential activity. It certainly does not reveal all its symbols (it consists of symbol precursors). Remember the important attitude you need to bring to bear on your generative metaphor, which I mentioned before: you need to tackle the metaphor *as though its meaning was already manifest in your life* and pretend that you know its riches. Applying this mindset will gate/direct your neural pathways in such a manner that the immediate constraints/current 'reality' are overcome as you evoke and visualize a future scenario, now.

Exercise: The metaphor animation questions now kick off

Now, armed with your transformative metaphor generated during Step 2 (Chapter 5), ensure that you have a big sheet of paper (at least A3 and preferably carton for durability) and drawing materials. Start creating your metaphor envelope or envelopes, drawing all the symbols as they emerge and how they are linked (use arrows). By 'envelope' I mean that you need to draw a frame on the paper to indicate what falls within the metaphor terrain, and what lies beyond (it could cover the whole sheet). Later on, further frames may become evident, e.g. when you feel that certain symbols within the envelope belong together. You can then draw a frame around them. Your initial frame then becomes a frame of frames or envelope of envelopes. The size, position and color of the symbols in itself are relevant and, just by changing their features, symbols will start 'revealing' more about themselves. (More on this later).

As a rule, stick to the images for as long as is possible when animating and hold ordinary thoughts in abeyance. See how the images change and unfold, facilitated by associations. Remember that you are engaging in a process of what Jung called 'active imagination', during which you turn inward to pick up on unfolding images and associations aligned with the transformative metaphor. You have to let go to enable your unconscious mind's image-making process. Words will inevitably tempt you to analyze and involve your ego and logic too much. This defies the process of animation (mainly visual). Let the symbols, in their guise as images, emerge at their own pace to bring insights and revelations *to* you. The bounded envelope and positively phrased metaphor will keep this process on track and focus the associations in a way that remains generative.

To summarize: symbols are pictures from within (unconscious), which reverberate through our senses taking shape as objects which are recognizable to us. First and foremost, the symbols bubble up in the mind's eye like an effervescent tablet does in a glass of water, and are not images from the external world.

The following task serves as a kick-off question to get the animation process going. This step is critical as it should populate your envelope, like water rushing into a dry riverbed after a big rain.

MAIN TASK: ASK YOURSELF THE FOLLOWING QUESTION:
NOW, what would be unfolding before my eyes if I WERE already achieving the outcomes contained in my transformative metaphor?
WRITE DOWN AND DRAW THE SYMBOLS.

Note: The word '*NOW*' in the above block focuses the mind onto a remembered future – making a prospective reality a current one. The word '*WERE*' allows for forward projection and the application of imagination to prospectively explore the scenario set out in the RGT metaphor.

- The above question is likely to reveal a number of symbols or even a progression of activities and a direction.
- If no symbols appear immediately, try not to force the

process – this would be counter-productive. Remember, the emergence of symbols arises outside your conscious awareness; they can't be forced. They are only recognized as such when you become aware of them. I like to think of the process as a paper, hot off the 'printing press of the unconscious', containing the outlines of cut-outs of images held in place by tiny needle-like contact points. You merely have to press on them to 'liberate' them from the background (paper) to make them come to life.

Tip: draw on your imagination by closing your eyes and opening your mind. (Flick your 'mental switch' from 'transmit' to 'receive'). Try to sense the symbols. Remain in a calm but attentive and receptive state, positioned between being awake and asleep, like in a waking dream. Scan what is happening in your mind's eye. You may find that symbols emerge or drift past your mind's eye like a movie. As these symbols emerge, record them (see task below). You may or may not know what they mean or how they fit in. If they don't yet fit into your envelope of existing symbols, simply put them on the margin for later reference and utilization.

Once the symbols (there will be more, going forward) have become evident, ensure you always do the following:

i.   *Write* them down on your big sheet of paper;
ii. *Draw* them in the color and form/size that they appear. They may be colored, achromatic or colorless (just the outline). Don't 'impose' your own color preferences based on what you may think looks 'nice', as the symbols and envelope environment will emerge in the appropriate form, shape and color when they manifest in your conscious mind. It is possible for the symbols to appear as words and/or images. If they appear as words, visualize what these words would be as pictures, sounds,

smells, tastes or feelings.

iii.   *Describe* what initial insights strike you as the meaning of the symbols become clear. Try not to think about the meaning – it should strike you out of the blue as new associations are made. Don't dwell on these initial insights even if tempted to do so. Remember, the attainment of the outcomes occurs within the metaphor domain/envelope, which uses symbols until the process is complete.

This should happen effortlessly and without interpretation. Then you can ask the following symbol animation questions (continue adding to and changing your envelope and symbols as you go through them). Important note: The questions below don't need to be asked strictly in the sequence in which they appear. Timing is important, so if a question doesn't take you forward, proceed with another one and then go back to the question(s) that had initially not yielded the desired outcomes. There is no such thing as a 'wrong' animation question – they all play an important role in achieving the outcomes you desire.

Task: Applying the metaphor animation questions to amplify the symbols

Now that you have put the facilitative question to your RGT metaphor and some symbols have appeared, put the following questions to the internal landscape you are engaging with:

If I WERE ALREADY ACHIEVING the scenario set out in my metaphor:

i.   What/who[4] (else) is it that I see, hear or feel?

ii.   How is the *quality* of what/who I see, hear or feel (light/dark; moving/still; loud/soft; textured/smooth; near/far; colored/achromatic)?

iii. How is that which I see, feel or hear related?[5]

iv. How does the total envelope or envelope encompassed by the metaphor look? In other words, what is the context; what happens around the symbols? (The metaphor envelope is a fertile internal psychic landscape largely generated unconsciously but made perceptible by the conscious mind as containing recognizable images.) You may want to monitor how it changes.

v. What changes in my emotions (if any) do I experience as I go through the exercise and why?

Tasks:

Amend your symbols in line with the response on the above questions, e.g. make them bigger or smaller; change their color based on what you 'see' and how they are related (use arrows); and add further symbols that emerge. Add any other information coming to you via your other senses, e.g. hearing, taste, smell, or touch. The idea is to make the symbols as 3-D and textured as possible. Remember, you are *anima*ting and amplifying, which may include movement. You are therefore merely *responding* to or contemplating changes in the mental picture, as opposed to *making* these changes. The animation process fuels new, spontaneous associations which also change the images, giving rise to new meanings and yet more associations. If necessary, add additional sheets of paper to your existing one (with staples or glue) for extra workspace.

Exploring the attributes/characteristics of the symbols

A highly useful question is one that seeks to explore the typology/characteristics of the symbols or their attributes. As each of the symbols become apparent, simply do the following for each of them:

Task: Ask the symbols the following questions:

'What [INSERT SYMBOL HERE] do you appear to be? What role do you fulfill, and why?'

Write the answers on the margin of the paper containing the metaphor envelope. You could draw an arrow from the description to the symbols within the envelope, e.g. 'This symbol's role is to...' You may find that the role(s) of some symbols change as you go forward, or that additional roles become clear. Alternatively, the clarity about their purpose may only strike you as the whole RGT metaphor matures. Simply be patient and try not to force the process.

This symbol typology eliciting question should provide an insight, which in turn would reveal the symbol's purpose, e.g. whether it is an explicit, conditional, enigmatic, dualistic or redemptive symbol. You may want to refer back to Chapter 3: "More on the Symbols' Role as Transformative Resources".

This will facilitate a process whereby new associations are formed. This may not be immediately apparent, but posing the question sets the stage for symbols to avail themselves and what meaning they intend to convey to you. (Follow-up questions around the symbols appear in a later section below).

Task: Determine your position vis-à-vis the metaphor[6]

i.   Are you *inside* the metaphor frame, looking through your own eyes at what is happening within the envelope and beyond? (associated, first-hand experience); and/or

ii.   Are you *outside* the metaphor envelope, looking *at* yourself in the envelope, like sitting on a park bench as an observer/fly on the wall? (disassociated, second-hand experience):

•   Describe the metaphor in your mind's eye and the emerging symbols for the two positions (associated and disassociated).

- See if the symbols and their attributes (*how* is that which you see, hear, feel, taste, or smell) change as you switch positions, and whether they bring about certain insights, which should strike you as ordinary thoughts. Make a note of this on your paper, referring to the symbol(s) to which this relates. Note: Insights, however, can also manifest as additional metaphors which then again need to be 'mined' for further clarity. What are you experiencing as an emotion(s) as you change from associated to disassociated, and vice versa? Write a short description of the emotion and which symbol(s) and position fostered it.

Tip: If you are actively involved in the metaphor envelope (see task below), you may find that you are *within* or even *on* a symbol. If this happens, look around you (turn around your own axis: 360 degrees) to look at the symbol you are closest to (or on) as well as other symbols, the envelope and way beyond in the distance to see what you notice.

Task: Determine whether you are active or passive
Are you doing something or looking at yourself doing something in the metaphor envelope?

i. What is it that you are doing?
ii. What is the impact of what you are doing on the metaphor envelope and its symbols?
iii. Do you feel that you wanted to engage with the symbols (active; associated) but that something was not yet in place or holding you back, like an impediment?

Write the above down your paper, linking it to the specific symbols or metaphor as a whole.

Comprehensiveness and maturation

I found that leaving the animation process for a while 'matures' it within your mind. It tends to become more comprehensive (see also later, 'metaphor time capsule'). Think of this like a good wine maturing in a cellar for a number of years, for its full potential to emerge. Visualize the envelope periodically and you may find that additional symbols arise spontaneously, particularly those resources symbols which are tacit or mysterious or depend on the envelope to come to fruition in a more comprehensive manner. Ensure you write down these impressions, tying them up with the symbols, associations and meanings that you are starting to make consciously.

MAIN TASKS:
DRAW A TABLE LIKE THE ONE BELOW ON A SEPARATE PIECE OF PAPER TO LEND SOME STRUCTURE TO YOUR ANIMATION PROCESS.
POPULATE IT WITH THE SYMBOLS (UNDER DONOR DOMAIN) AND INSIGHTS (UNDER RECIPIENT DOMAIN). (IT IS BEST TO DRAW THE SYMBOLS TO KEEP THE PROCESS SENSORY.)
ENSURE YOU CHANGE IT/ADD TO IT AS THE ANIMATION PROCESS PROGRESSES.

A table similar to the one below (example) will help you capture what you have achieved thus far. As the decoding process is cumulative, this information will become the basis for the next steps. I'll use the case study of 'plain sailing' by way of an example. It contains the narrative of the person who came up with 'My life is plain sailing'.

DONOR DOMAIN: ANIMATED SYMBOLS			RECIPIENT DOMAIN	
List/draw the symbols here (what) & how they relate to other	List symbol characteristics here and your position (in picture / looking at picture)	Type of resource	Insights/ associations and constraints	Emotions
Boat. Related to everything; and everything to it.	Yacht; medium sized, white Associated & disassociated	Explicit: 'vehicle' to get to plain sailing	Also a 'womb' – a place to grow psychologically, but need for self-reliance (unlike fetus).	Warm; protected; safe.
Sails. Related to all.	Large & inflated	Explicit resource: Harnesses wind.	Direct your sails to the wind (insight).	Exhilaration
Port holes	Large. In cabin, looking through portholes (associated).	Mysterious / Tacit	No clarity yet – to be unpacked further.	
Wind. Related to all.	Strong. Wind and water spray on face. Hair blown back (associated).	Explicit resource; "Fuel" to get to destination (extraneous; out of my control).	Can even use head-wind to make progress. This is a major insight: obstacles as resources. One cannot expect 'plain sailing" all the time!	-
Ocean. Related to all.	Blue in the harbor; black outside.	Linkage between current & desired (destination). Medium through which to attain the RGT metaphor.	My freedom; my prison cell. Ambivalence. Can I handle the good with the bad? Can I go the distance & prevail?	Trepidation
People	Immediate family	Explicit	Others are 'wind in my sails', but they must also get what they want. Related to progress and reduction of anxiety and fear.	Guilt
Harbor	Calm and protected. I see myself looking at myself on the boat, securely moored in harbor, softly moving with the ripples of the waves (disassociated).	Explicit	Somehow the harbor reflects core values. You need a solid foundation to move from, and to return to, if things get rough. Sense of knowing that all will be alright even if destination is not clear. Related to ensuring that plain sailing is 'true' and really rooted in self, rather than the push and pull of the world, other's expectations and the lure of the material. I am able to resist making myself feel better by buying material stuff.	Contented Calm
Anchor	Large / life-size. Looking underwater to see why boat isn't moving – visual / (associated).	Dualistic and Conditional	The anchor is a constraint at the moment. But it serves a purpose – keeps me safe, but keeps me from moving.	Frustration at not moving. Fear of moving.

Table 6.1: Types of symbols and insights/associations yielded
through animation: Example

Task: Identifying and prioritizing symbols for further animation

From the table above (populated with *your* own symbols, narrative and insight), determine:

i. If you get a sense that there may be symbols that are not yet present. The animation process and working with the symbols is likely to yield more symbols.

ii. Which symbols need to be animated further (keep in mind that new symbols may arise at any time) to reveal:

   a. themselves as resources; and

   b. their purpose/intent, thus fostering the remedial, generative or transformative processes.

iii. Constraints, which can include oppositional dilemmas, such as being in 'two minds' about something or facing two 'equal' options, the indecision of which immobilizes you (more on this in Chapter 7).

Second Round of Symbol Animation: 'Above-the-Senses' Editing

In order to populate the metaphor envelope further through the elicitation of additional symbols and the clarification of their purpose/role, try the following:

Vantage point

Sometimes in films, the camera 'spins' around an object or person, providing a view from all angles, or is positioned bottom-up or top-down. Certain films are edited in such a manner that the viewer gets to see different perspectives (stories) sequentially. This provides different perspectives, often resulting in very different understandings, outcomes and emotional responses. Somebody who looked positively guilty from one perspective may appear from another to be a kind Samaritan assisting a victim, or vice versa. Your position would be the different camera angles positioned around the metaphor envelope, which is really a three-dimensional, objective and textured inner reality. The profound thing is that the position of the observer (you) does not merely provide a view but will actually *alter* the symbols during the animation process, how they come to life and what they will mean to you. Different perspectives will determine *how* symbols appear and *what* symbols appear. This is in line with the objectives of the animation process which yields remedial, generative or transformative outcomes.

Therefore you need to shift positions vis-à-vis the metaphor envelope and determine how this alters the features ('how') of the symbols and which additional ones may appear (or disappear) and how this facilitates progression toward the outcome(s) locked up in the RGT metaphor. You may find that this is a process whereby you constantly have to gauge if you are on track and on the way to attaining the desired outcome. If you change your vantage point and find yourself drifting off the 'sweet spot', go back to where you were and then try another angle and see what this reveals.

Tasks:

- In your mind's eye, place yourself into the various positions vis-à-vis the metaphor envelope and then carefully record your impressions from each of the angles (see figure below), including views from the front; back; left; right; top; bottom and positions in-between.
- Always look up and down when you change your positions. Remember, even though the envelope and its symbols are emerging imprints of your inner world, treat it as if it were a 3-D virtual reality, which has a 'sky' and 'earth'; day and night. (Just think of the movie, "The Truman Show").
- Note how this changes and augments the characteristics of each of the symbols/RGT metaphor as a whole. Change/add to the symbols, using your color pens. Also make note of any insights or new associations that could strike you at the time. Ensure you draw/write all of this down on your paper/table.

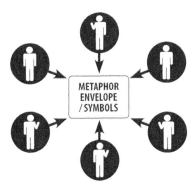

Figure 6.1: Positions vis-à-vis the metaphor envelope and symbols

Task: Zooming in, zooming out

Imagine you were looking through a camera with a powerful zoom:

i.   Are you zooming in on detail or zooming out to capture the whole metaphoric envelope and beyond?

ii. If you were to *zoom out,* allowing the full metaphoric envelope to come into view:
  * how does this change your experience?
  * is there anything or anybody that you become aware of in, or *beyond* the immediate metaphor envelope?
  * is something else happening or is somebody else doing something in, or beyond the envelope? How does this impact on the envelope and the symbols?
  * how are these things or people related?

iii. If you were to *zoom in,* looking at the finest level of detail:
  * what does this reveal about the individual symbols?
  * how does this change your experience?

Carefully record your observations and which symbol(s) this has a bearing on.

Task: Accentuating/diminishing the features[7] ('how') of the symbols

Take each of the symbols in your mind's eye which have not 'revealed' their purpose or intent, and do the following:

i. What you see

- Make them larger or smaller in your mind's eye, and then see what happens.
- Change their location in the metaphor envelope and see if/how this has an impact.
- Make them brighter or dimmer and see what happens.
- If they are panoramic, place a frame around them; if they are framed, remove the frame in your mind's eye and see what happens.
- 'Shift time' from a daylight setting to night and vice versa (including dusk/dawn), and introduce artificial light (lamp; candles) at night. This (including shadows cast by the symbols on the 'wall' of your envelope) could reveal additional attributes of the symbols or your relationship with them.

ii. What you hear

If the symbols make a sound, 'turn' the sounds they make louder or softer and see if this yields a result in the sense of further clarity. It is possible that a tune emerges (rather than individual sounds), much like a movie soundtrack. As you would know from watching movies, the music plays an important role in accentuating certain scenes and drawing attention away from others. The music rings-in the changes and 'sets the tone' for the movie and thereby plays an important role in the emotional experience of the audience. It is true for both the symbols constituting the metaphor and movie music that changing the volume and type of music changes how we pay attention and the meaning we make (notably at an emotional level) of certain scenes (symbols) compared to others.

iii. What you feel

- See what happens if you engage with symbols by pulling them or pushing against them. They may 'resist' these attempts, or be amenable to being pulled closer and into an 'inner circle' of other symbols. This is important to reveal certain interrelationships and grouping of symbols. If the symbols are not amenable to being 'introduced' to others, ask each of them what would have to happen for them to be comfortable being introduced.
- Explore the shape and textures of symbols and see what this reveals. You merely need to visualize (as a proxy for your sense organ of touch) how symbols feel, and they will reveal more about their purpose/utility as resources.
- If you stand on symbols, sense what you feel under your feet or body and whether this reveals (1) certain insights about the symbols; and (2) your relationship with them. You need to be associated at this time (experience the symbols through your own eyes, rather than looking at your interaction with them from a distance).

iv. What you smell or taste

You may notice that the symbols evoke smells or tastes that could have meaning. Alternatively, your activities within or vis-à-vis the RGT metaphor envelope and its symbols could make you experience certain smells or tastes.

Ensure that you carefully record all of the above impressions on your piece of paper, showing linkages with/between the symbols.

Task: Looking 'into' and 'under' symbols

You can further animate symbols by:

- Looking *into* them when they appear as containers or vessels, e.g. boats, bottles, boxes. Often these 'hollow' symbols have things in them (which are potentially further symbols requiring animation). Emotional metaphors often include containers, e.g. 'He was boiling over with anger' (the person being some sort of 'vessel').

- Looking underneath them – symbols can be lifted like ordinary objects to reveal additional attributes that would move you to new insights, generate new perspectives or further the process toward the final frontier of transformation. If you get a sense that there is more to symbols, look underneath them. If there is a boat or other floating object in your metaphor envelope, see what is revealed if you look underneath. If it is a body of water, you may want to go underneath the surface and see what you discover that may create certain insights or inspiration. (Imagine that you are wearing goggles and 'peek' underneath the surface.)

Ensure that you carefully record all of the above impressions on your piece of paper, showing linkages with/between the symbols.

Testing different permutations of relationships between symbols

Explore further linkages/relationships between the symbols and between the latter and the RGT metaphor as a whole, since some may have escaped your attention previously. See if this provides some insights or understanding which did not exist previously. Record these relationships, the meaning of the symbols and then the insights you derive from them.

Task: 'Ask' symbols about their intent or purpose

Further to the above steps, simply 'ask' the symbols which you are still unclear about:

i.   what their intent or purpose may be (what they would like to bring about within the metaphorical domain and vis-à-vis other symbols) and *why*. If nothing is revealed, 'ask' the symbols to *pretend* that they knew their purpose. This 'moves' time forward and creates a future possibility for your unconscious mind to latch onto and generate creative options that may break a stalemate and accelerate the animation process.

ii. what *they* see and where to/how this is going (remember they are 'looking inward', into your collective unconscious). Tell them that you really want to know.

iii. whether they can execute their intent/purpose ('readiness'), and if not, *what is required for them to do this*. The question, 'What is required?' seeks to uncover conditions that may have to be met. These could be conditions within the metaphoric envelope, relating to the symbols, or conditions that have to be met by the metaphor 'beneficiary' (YOU).

The above questions are tailored to get more information about symbols as tacit, situational and conditional resources. Remember to address the symbols in a personal fashion and not as objects. They are alive and manifest as processes.

Exploring linkages: Second round of symbol animation

It is important to again explore the *linkages* between the symbols subjected to additional animation, including the exploration of their intent and purpose (see above). You would recall that changes in one symbol (or part) can change other parts and reorganize the whole. The highest probability of sustainable change is when the fundamental organization of the metaphor envelope changes spontaneously.

Task: 'Shift' time: backward and forward framing of time

Like all life-experiences, one would expect the metaphoric envelope to be tied into a time-line too. There should be events leading up to the 'events' within and beyond the metaphor frame. Since the metaphor is generative or transformative, something should happen next. If nothing happens/can happen, this is usually because certain conditions or requirements have to be met and brought to bear on the metaphoric envelope. It is important to explore these changes within the context of the metaphor envelope and therefore the 'reality' of the symbols, rather than engaging in thoughts or 'ordinary' narrative. The reason for this is to keep the rational mind (which has been shown to have limited purview) out of the picture and to let the unconscious and symbols do the transformative work. As has been explained, changes in the metaphor envelope – as a microcosm of you – will result in changes in mind and brain, in the form of a mental 'retro-fit'.

Tasks: Put the following two questions to your generative metaphor:

i.   How did that which happened prior, shape the *metaphoric envelope*?

ii. What happens going forward and how does this change things[8] within the metaphor envelope or envelope of envelopes? If you put this question to the symbol, insight or constraint around the symbol, you might get the following 'replies':

   a. 'Nothing happens, going forward.' This may mean that the future in the metaphor envelope is not instrumental or not yet ready to transpire. If this is the case, re-apply the metaphor animating questions to further unpack the RGT metaphor. This may complete the scenario-based process set out in the metaphor. If an expanded animation process still does not create in you a sense of clarity or transformation, do the following:

- Travel forward in time to a year or so from now, to the day (the future is in front of you; the present/past behind);

- Visualize yourself as a one-person 'welcoming committee', with flowers and champagne in hand, waiting for the person you expect to arrive, like at a railway station or airport. You need to make a 180 degree turn in your mind's eye and face what would now be the past from where your 'double' will appear (you are both in the past and the future);

- Now visualize your 'double' appearing after s/he has attained the possibilities or scenario(s) set out in RGT or after these possibilities have transpired;

- Welcome your double and ask him/her to share what has happened in the RGT metaphor. Note: *first* inquire about the symbols once animated (their features and the progression or story-line within the envelope). *Then* ask about the learnings, insights and feelings which your double has assimilated based on the animation process materializing. Because your double has seen the RGT metaphor become a reality, he/she will typically report in the *past tense*. Also look at your double: how do they look after this journey? Are they refreshed and wiser? (Remember this is really YOU. The purpose of you as an observer is to get a clear view of, and assimilate your learnings.)

b. 'Nothing *can/wants to happen*, going forward.' This may mean that certain conditions are yet to be met at the level of the symbols or the metaphor as a whole for 'movement' or progress to take place. If oppositional dilemmas are at the root of the problem, proceed to the next chapter. If no oppositional dilemmas are apparent, intensify the animation process, using the questions set out in this chapter or revert back to (a), above.

Those of you who have seen the film *A Night at the Museum*, with Ben Stiller, will recall that the figures (both humans and animals) in the museum come to life at night. They start to interact with each other and fulfill certain functions that achieve certain ends. The animation process is much the same. In the beginning you only have the metaphor with its symbol precursors (these are the actual words that appear in the metaphor). Once you start animating the symbols within the metaphor, you start bringing them to life – you 'awaken' them. Once this has happened, the symbols start having exploratory 'relationships' with each other, much like people that meet others for the first time. It will become clear how and why they are related and which functions they mutually fulfill for each other and in the service of the process you are pursuing. Hence, the markers of the success of the animation process are as follows:

- the symbols in the envelope have 'come to life' and there is a *progression* of events much like a movie. There is a clear sense of a beginning and an end. Once the movie is produced (that is to say, your animation process is complete), the scenes constituting it remain the same as you 'rewind' and 'look at the movie' (metaphor in motion) again. What doesn't remain the same is the meaning and associations you make as you look at it over and over. The meaning changes (or is augmented) as you start recognizing additional aspects within the scenes (these could be objects or people). You may want to look at your metaphor envelope a few times by 'pausing' each symbol again and then reapply the metaphor animation questions. The story as animated will also contain much of the meaning, alluding to prior events and also what could happen, going forward.

• some significant insight/clarity and inspiration would have struck you based on the animation process. This would provide some remedial, generative or even trans-formative 'material' that otherwise may not have come to mind through logic, 'thinking harder' about or resisting problems or where you want to go.

Task: How to create a metaphor time-capsule

The metaphor animation process is like a door that opens outward. Leaning against and pushing on it will do no good. It may even be counter-productive, as the symbols can't emerge. You can't hurry a profound thing. Client experience with the metaphor animation process has shown that it is fruitful to step away from the process for a while to let it mature. The idea of a metaphor time-capsule is based on events during my childhood in a small, dusty Namibian town called Okahandja (if you want, you can Google it). As kids we loved to create secret time-capsules by burying our most prized possessions, like marbles; toys; air gun pellets, etc. in a shallow hole in the ground, usually in a dry riverbed. We then covered the hole with a piece of window pane, so that the content remained visible like a shop display window. Thereafter we completely covered the glass with sand, leaving a marker for later retrieval. After months, we would go back to retrieve our 'treasures'. The experience was thoroughly mystical and magical, like having created a parallel universe moving forward independently but somehow connected to us. This was particularly the case when we had forgotten about the time-capsules only to rediscover them by chance many months (and sometimes years) later. It was as if the content had changed and became energized, or perhaps it had changed us? Everything had new meaning and value; we felt a stronger emotional affinity for the content, like an oyster bringing forth a brilliant pearl.

It was only later that the deeply symbolic nature of the time-capsule process (as an incubator for the animation process) dawned on me and I started applying it to metaphor animation. Earth is associated with origins; relinquishing something treasured (by our egos) to the earth mother (collective unconscious) for reorientation and maturation, only for the ego to later 'liberate' it and take it into the light of consciousness for enhanced personal growth, strength and maturity.

When you have progressed some way with the metaphor animation process, do the following as a private, secret ritual (in the order as indicated):

i.   Stick your metaphor drawing on a carton. You could also roll up your piece of paper containing your RGT metaphor envelope and place it in a cigar tube/carton roll (use a tin foil/wax paper roll).

ii. Now, place the metaphor drawing in a hole in the garden or any location you may choose. It is best to use a plastic container to protect the contents. After putting the box in place, cover the hole with a piece of window pane/clear plastic and then put a thin layer of sand/soil over it. Place a marker by the hole for future identification. (If you have a dog, perhaps bury the time-capsule in another location.)

iii. Thank your collective unconscious for revealing to you the change that you desire.

iv. After some weeks or months, go back to the time-capsule and carefully sweep away the sand/soil on the glass. Be receptive to the feelings, impressions and insights that strike you as the contents slowly come to light. Prepare yourself for quite a powerful feeling. Ensure you write down/draw any insights, change or transformation as well as additional symbols and/or linkages between them that you may want to add to your drawing.

Tip: when your animation process gets stuck under any of the sections/tasks covered thus far, use the following 'time-shifter' question:

'*HOW* is that which is just about to happen next?'

Again, you are interested not such much in *what* happens, but *how*, so as to stay at the higher level of how symbols appear – their features. Remember, they don't necessarily have fixed, universal meanings, but are indefinite *possibilities* and *processes* to achieve the change you want. Symbols as processes should not be reified and turned into static objects.

Summary

✓ You would have become more competent in understanding and applying the metaphor animation questions and which of these questions would be most applicable, given the state of animation.

✓ Your metaphor envelope should be *richer, with more symbols* having appeared than were contained in the initial generative metaphor (including the symbol precursors). It is strongly suggested that you draw your symbols, *which* of these are related (indicate by drawing arrows) and *how*. You can even introduce little notes or 'speech-bubbles' to remind you of the nature of the interaction between the various symbols and what insight they provided.

✓ The metaphor envelope should not be static, but animated – there should be some relationship/interaction between the symbols. It should be reasonably clear to you *how* and *why* they are interacting.

✓ You should have a sense of which symbols are resources and what type of resources they are (refer to the list and definitions in Chapter 3).

✓ The animation of the symbols would have brought you to some insights, possibly even profound ones, including those resulting in transformation and sense of purpose. Some questions may remain unanswered or new questions may have arisen due to the animation process.

✓ You may have become aware of constraints. Remember, you tackled the animation process as if the scenario painted by the metaphor had already been attained and that its meaning were clear. In your mind's eye you may be actively enacting the metaphor's meaning, although in your heart of hearts you know that not everything is in place to achieve that prospective (rehearsed) reality.

✓ The animation process should provide clarity in the form of symbols rather than ordinary thoughts/narrative. You may want to prioritize the ones that you find most striking or mysterious and apply the animation process set out in this chapter to them. Remind yourself that animation is essentially a content-free approach, which deals with the 'how' rather than 'what'. All change happens within the envelope, but will strike you in the form of ordinary narrative (insights and associations).

✓ You may start realizing that the burning questions or obstacles you had cease to exist or lose their significance as the animation process advances. This is a sign of a Level 2 change, as you may not be getting better answers because your questions are starting to change.

✓ The animation process you have gone through thus far may have highlighted oppositional dilemmas. These can include:

• being in 'two minds' about going with a particular course

of action, resulting in an inner hiatus ('part' of you wants to; another doesn't);

- a tug-of-war due to the perceived consequences of two courses of actions, e.g. you feel that if you do/get something you want, others may not get what they want and vice versa. In both instances perceived consequences could include guilt about being 'selfish' (when doing something for 'Self' and thereby 'disenfranchising' others); or resentfulness (even anger) for doing something for others and short-changing yourself. The emotional consequences can be quite significant, but as the next chapter shows a useful (even necessary or critical) catalyst for change.

Oppositional dilemmas often occur at the brink or tipping point of significant change/transformation because of the high emotional intensity that accompanies them. This energy can be harnessed to elicit resource symbols that will foster a distinct break with what you have experienced up to now and drive the process of achieving remarkable results. Therefore, the next chapter is entirely and extensively dedicated to oppositional dilemmas, as these are quite common but also to be expected once the animation process starts to gain momentum.

Think of animation as an archeological dig to extract a fossil embedded in stone, frozen in time. A single fragment may appear as a clue on the basis of which you have to visualize how this fits into a bigger picture to guide your step-wise excavation process, preventing damage to what you are after. Proceed with the same care and patience as a paleoanthropologist would, with brush and fine hand-tools. You may find a bone fragment here; brush the sand away; uncover a digit there; blow the sand away; see a whole hand, and finally a skull and whole skeleton may emerge.

More work may have to be done if you have hit the

seemingly unsolvable dilemmas or impasses as discussed. This is the subject of the next chapter.

ENDNOTES

1 This seeks to 'tease out' the metaphor and its sub-components to reveal their latent meaning or resources required for change.

2 The subconscious mind [the narrower, Freudian conception; Jung: unconscious mind (wider concept including the collective unconscious mind)] processes some '20 *million* stimuli per second vs. the paltry 40 stimuli (nerve impulses) per second by the conscious mind in the same second' (Lipton, 2005).

3 Some informed by or adapted from Lawley and Tomkins (2000).

4 Remember that other people can also be symbols and serve as resources in your metaphor envelope.

5 This is aimed at exploring the relationship between the symbols within the metaphor frame.

6 Associated/disassociated: If you find yourself being an observer (disassociated) and that this prevents you from taking ownership of your needs or dreams, then enter the metaphor frame. Looking at the metaphor through your own eyes increases the emotional intensity of the experience and makes it more real, thus contributing to the animation of the envelope and your relationship with it. Furthermore, being an active participant allows you to reshuffle the envelope and contribute to bringing the symbols to life, thereby securing clarity, insight, change or transformation.

7 NLP techniques (Bandler and Grinder) involve working with the features (or so-called sub-modalities) of what we perceive through our five senses (light/dark would be sub-modalities of what we see). The cardinal difference here is

that we are not dealing with mere sensory features but with symbols that form part of a metaphoric *whole*. Symbols are no longer ordinary sensory experiences, but already *experiences of experiences* that make sense within the context of the metaphor. Furthermore, symbols are trans-personal and not mere individual memories or perceptions. Whilst some metaphor animation techniques overlap with those of NLP, the objectives and outcomes differ vastly from those of NLP. Yet some NLP techniques appear to work well when animating the RGT metaphor and the genius of the two NLP originators is hereby acknowledged with gratitude.

8   The word 'things' is intentionally vague in order for the unconscious mind to generate its own meaning by going through a search function.

Chapter 7

Resolving Polarities at the Brink of Transformation

The intuitive mind is a sacred gift; the rational mind its faithful servant. We have created a society that honors the servant and has forgotten the gift.
Albert Einstein

Purpose of this chapter

If you got this far, congratulations – it means that the animation process has made you hit some sort of internal conflict or polarization within the metaphor envelope that resonates with something in your life. This chapter on polarities or oppositional dilemmas will also reveal the most fundamental mechanisms that may be at work in the manner in which symbols avail themselves as resources.

The purpose of this chapter is to clarify oppositional dilemmas by way of example and assist you in understanding your own. It provides some refinements of the extensive list of metaphor animation questions set out in the previous chapter. The understanding, based on this chapter, is for you to reapply the metaphor animation questions to arrive at a resolution/reconciliation of any oppositional dilemmas. Please note that animation makes symbols emerge even in the absence of polarities discussed in this chapter. However, the emotional energy associated with the challenge or problem that first motivated you to translate it into a negative metaphor and then the RGT metaphor, should be sustained and not allowed to ebb away. The energy helps lift your unconscious milieu reflected in the RGT metaphor and edge it toward consciousness so that you can more fruitfully engage with it. It therefore provides critical motivational energy to engage with the symbols and learn from them. According to Jung (1995), 'only here, in life on earth, where the opposites clash together can the general level of consciousness be raised' (p.343). No pain, no gain.

Introduction to Oppositional Dilemmas

One can distinguish between ordinary or simple obstacles to change which manifest as a result of the metaphor animation process. These ordinary obstacles may simply be the result of the animation process not having fully come to fruition. You then need to engage with your RGT metaphor and symbols again, with renewed enthusiasm and resolve using the animation questions from the previous chapter. For example, a change in observer location could reveal symbol attributes that were not evident previously, but could prove to be instrumental in creating much-needed movement toward the prospective scenario inherent in the RGT metaphor. Then there are the more complex obstacles to change, which can be as follows:

Internal

This is when the animation process of the RGT metaphor has been exhausted and the way forward is clear, but you find yourself conflicted in principle and not because of the options before you. This is when a 'part' of you wants to make the change, and another wants to stay put. This is an oppositional dilemma within the Self, which can be metaphorically expressed as 'I am in two minds about it.' Again, the answer can be found within the metaphor envelope as the symbols are particularly apt at resolving oppositional dilemmas – in this case, two states of mind. A resource symbol(s) has to be animated which is able to clarify or unify these opposites at a higher (transcendent) or more abstract level, bringing you to new insights. Of course, there is another alternative, such as doing nothing or shifting attention away from the dilemma and thereby superseding the 'two minds' at conflict with each other. However, you may eventually find yourself getting back to the point where you face the conflict of minds yet again. More sustainable and fundamental solutions are therefore desirable.

External

In the case of external obstacles to change, you may experience the following during the process of engaging with the RGT metaphor:

a. You have hit an *obstacle* which seems insurmountable. This can be fairly easily remedied by tackling the animation process with renewed optimism, enthusiasm and energy. Expand and deepen the symbols to unlock more resources that could prove to overcome the obstacle that appears at first. However, the suspended animation may be because of obstacles which include b. and c. below, which are harder to deal with.

b. You experience a quagmire, whereby you face *two equally appealing (or unappealing) alternatives*, which strike you during the animation process. This is what people may mean if they speak about 'a rock and a hard place'. This essentially portrays an oppositional dilemma, which can bring the animation process to a grinding halt. This should be more rare, as the overarching metaphor is generative – a frame for creating new options rather than trying 'to fix' old problems, which would be the general purview of therapy. The latter would attempt to get you 'back to baseline' psychologically, whilst metaphor animation seeks to get you beyond baseline or to completely redefine the current baseline and/or your attitude towards it. However, the challenges involved in pursuing options sketched in the RGT metaphor vs.

perpetuating the status quo (as set out in the negative metaphor) may manifest as an oppositional dilemma.

c. You find that the solutions or options generated through animation and the 'work' of resource symbols provides short-term relief, with the problem getting worse again later. This is best reflected in the notion of 'the more things change, the more they stay the same', or 'yesterday's solution becomes today's problem'.[1] As discussed earlier, any system 'wants' to stay within the 'normal' range of functioning (refer to 'spider web'), thereby ensuring its ongoing existence. However, paradoxically this also prevents growth and change, resulting in discontentment, discomfort or frustration either way. This obtains in both the system of mind (you) and wider systems, such as you in the context of meaningful others. Bradshaw[2] has written extensively about this self-perpetuating nature of family systems, where the linkages between the members become increasingly rigid. No matter what changes are made, the system seems to revert back to baseline[3] (which is often an unbearable place for those involved). Hence, 'the more things change, the more they stay the same'. Later, the collective energy goes only into perpetuating the system at the expense of the well-being and growth of the individuals, which is necessary for a functional and generative system. This process is often tied into oppositional dilemmas, which are discussed below, whereby going with any one option available creates unwanted outcomes (or perceived outcomes), thus perpetuating lack of movement or 'cycling' through the options, but always ending up at the starting point. (Generating a RGT metaphor which characterizes the relationship[4] as if it already were how both partners would want it to be, or what it could be, yields the same possibilities for change and transformation that the RGT metaphor offers individuals.)

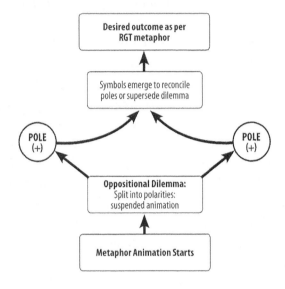

Figure 7.1: Polarities emerge as animation brings the RGT metaphor to a head

As the above figure shows, the animation process comes to a halt as you become conscious of an oppositional dilemma or dilemmas (opposing poles which repel one another: (+)). You are at that moment aware of both polarities, which effectively dilute the energy necessary for the attainment of the RGT metaphor outcome(s), but at the same time contain a potential. This is why there can be no further effective progression toward this outcome, until such time that a symbol(s) avails itself that can reconcile these poles or completely supersede them (rise above the oppositional dilemma). The energy that was previously diluted is now recombined and intensified and sufficient to achieve the RGT metaphor outcome (the potential unfolds).

Oppositional dilemmas as energy for transformation

From all of the above, those characterized by an oppositional dilemma, i.e. (1) either not *wanting/being able to choose* (internal conflict); or (2) not *wanting the choices available* (or wanting them both) (external dilemma), can be the most challenging (and are often very common). However, the animated symbols also have their work cut out in terms of oppositional dilemmas. Furthermore, oppositional dilemmas usually occur at the cusp of transformation. My work has confirmed Jung's view that the tension that accompanies them is in fact necessary for transformation. This is much like a butterfly that has to struggle its way out of its cocoon in order to develop its wings so that it can fly. Any premature interference from the outside (such as tearing the cocoon open to 'free the butterfly') will result in its wings not developing, which makes it unable to meet the demands of flying.

So, if your metaphor envelope (or envelope of envelopes) starts to show polarities, you are making great progress. Rejoice, even if the tension is hard to deal with – you are busy strengthening your mental wings and becoming stronger, much like the butterfly struggling to free itself. Remedial and generative outcomes are usually more easily achieved just by animating the symbols further. Transformation on the other hand is big-picture stuff and quite fundamental, so much so that behavioral change follows effortlessly and without much conscious effort or input.

Oppositional dilemmas don't arise as long as we focus our attention on/are aware of one pole (in ourselves or in terms of choices) at a time, i.e. as we become conscious of and identify[5] with it, the other drifts into the background (unconscious) and vice versa. This alternating process doesn't present much of a problem, until metaphor animation makes us consciously aware of *both* polarities and we feel that they are somehow 'weighted' equally. This weighting and not being able/willing to move, or wanting to move into one direction *and* the other concurrently, puts the metaphor (and by implication, ourselves) into a state of *suspended animation* or *hiatus*. This suspension of the alternating process and concurrent awareness creates quite formidable tension and emotionality, which you may experience if your animation process uncovers oppositional dilemmas. When people find themselves in these sorts of oppositional dilemmas, they often use a metaphor that conveys this quite strongly, e.g. 'I'm damned if I do, damned if I don't'; or 'My head says X, and my heart says Y.' The figures below should make things clearer.

In the first figure below, the oppositional dilemma has not yet come to a head within the metaphor landscape. This may be because the symbols that are instrumental to revealing the oppositional dilemma have not yet appeared or the animation process has not advanced to a stage where oppositional dilemmas arise. You may still be in the phase where insights strike you that are of a remedial or generative nature. Prior to the oppositional dilemma, you are becoming aware of various impressions, which enter your conscious mind in an alternating fashion. There is no indication of a conflict or dilemma. In the first figure below, this is reflected with 'A' becoming conscious, then 'vacating' the space, which is then taken up by 'B', and vice versa. The alternating movement is probably fueled by your ego fixating on each of the poles in turn, in the hope of finding a resolution to the oppositional dilemma. If your ego focuses on one pole too much, the other arises as a form of unconscious compensation or by way of supplementing consciousness and to restore balance. (Jung's idea of how the psyche functions. A clarifying quote often attributed to Jung in fact is, 'what you resist, persists'). However, as soon as this has happened, the process reverses itself due to 'A' pushing down (see arrow) to keep 'B' from becoming conscious, whilst 'B', competing for conscious attention and to restore balance, pushes up (see upward arrow).

Either way, a resolution doesn't arise, because the problem

cannot be solved with the same mind that created it (to paraphrase Einstein) – it needs to be transformed at a 'higher' level or in a different mental dimension.

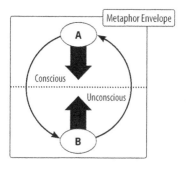

Figure 7.2: Poles alternating between the conscious and unconscious mind

Then, the animation process brings the situation to a head whereby you suddenly become aware of the oppositional dilemma. This process is accompanied by quite a signficant tension between the two poles, which in the figure below is indicated by the horizonal double-headed arrow. In order to understand this tension, think about holding a thick spring in both hands, twisting it downward until it forms a 'U' (this is the butterfly practicing and strengthening its wings). It is hard to hold the spring in this position and you would be aware of the energy you expend to twist the spring. Usually it is easiest just to let go and the spring reverts to its resting position. This again starts the unwanted '(dis)comfort zone' resulting from suspended alternation of the poles of opposition, something that can be hard to endure. If you were to hold on, the tensions would be directed into your body and mind – exerting strain (the price) but also building muscle (the reward).

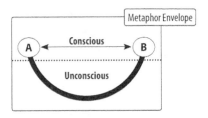

Figure 7.3: Pole alternation suspended: both conscious at the
same time

Within the context of the metaphor animation process the
energy that is generated when both poles are conscious simulta-
neously plays a critical role. The energy has nowhere to go[6] but
into the unconscious.[7] In this regard, the fact that you are
working within the 'sealed' and defined context of the metaphor
envelope (or envelope of envelopes) is an important consider-
ation. It allows for dilemmas to be worked out at the level of
symbols that relate to each other and the metaphor as a whole
and are 'retro-fitted' into your mental operations as the
metaphor beneficiary, providing the desired outcomes. You
would recall that the changes in the metaphor landscape are
brought to bear on you by way of remedy, generative dynamics
or transformation.

Therefore, the formidable energy and tension that is created
due to oppositional issues can be channeled into the envelope.
Harnessed by the symbols (and visible as images in your
envelope), the tension bolsters the animation process. It imbues
you as the animator with imagination, fostering renewal, change
or transformation rather than being displaced[8] through
conscious, narrative interaction with the world, thereby losing
its constructive role.

The energized envelope results in the appearance, from the
unconscious, of new symbols or existing symbols availing
themselves as resources. Remember that symbols transform
unconscious mental energy into something useful and

constructive. In particular, the resource symbols would be necessary to supersede the oppositional dilemma, resulting in reconciliation at the level of transformation. This ensuing process of transformation may not result in you choosing one option over another, or going with one 'part' of the mind (if you are 'in two minds'). Transformation may work at the level of the *consequences* you face by going/not going with a certain option (or pole). This can result in the oppositional dilemma no longer being an issue because a more fundamental (or higher level) change encompasses and, at the same time, supersedes the oppositional dilemma, thereby bringing resolution. This is the mental 're-set button' I mentioned earlier. Given that transformation is at the level of the Self (your total psyche), you may no longer perceive the oppositional dilemma to exist. Or, it simply no longer matters! This is because transformation happens at the level of the totality of the metaphor (and with that, your psyche, as the two are inextricably linked in the envelope). One could speak of a total 'over-*whole*' rather than overhaul.

In the figure below, this is shown by an arrow pointing downwards toward the unconscious. Think about this arrow as an inverted ice-cream cone that you stick into a big container of 'hundreds and thousands' (multi-colored, sweet, cake decorations). These hundreds and thousands (symbols) cling to the ice-cream because of their properties and the stickiness of the ice-cream (both therefore have characteristics to be drawn to each other). Through their contact, both are transformed. Similarly, the symbols, pregnant with meaning, are drawn upwards due to the energy released from the arrow into the unconscious (due to the oppositional dilemma and resultant suspended animation). Or, putting it differently, the arrows are like pouring lighter fluid (energy from the oppositional tension) onto smoldering coals (unconscious), with flames (symbols) shooting upward as they have nowhere else to go. The arrow pointing upwards is a conduit for the symbols that are necessary to work on the oppositional dilemma. Yet another analogy is to think of hitting a drum with 'smarties' (small chocolate candies) on it; as you hit the drum (energy release), the smarties fly upward and are 'caught' by the conscious mind – this is the percussive equivalent of the visual analogies above.

You may find that the symbols appear as *ordinary 'objects' with an extraordinary transformative 'payload'*, which means something for you subjectively. The symbols will therefore possibly 'disguise' themselves as objects that resonated with you throughout your life and have special significance. They are therefore well placed to serve as carriers or mediums for transformative meaning, as the material from the archetypes in the collective unconscious can attach itself to them. Being recognizable, they are more amenable to your ego and less likely to be viewed critically and potentially blocked, which would make it impossible for their *muti* (African term, meaning 'medicine') to do its magic. They are therefore like "Trojan horses" that on the surface are benign-looking and instantaneously recognizable and therefore allowed 'in' (into the conscious mind), but pack an awesome punch, once they release their magic. As they hit consciousness, they discard their cloaks.

Emily Dickinson (in Edelman, 2004), summarizes very well the idea that we have to stretch our minds to embrace a greater reality of connectivity (e.g. by using metaphor):

The Brain is wider than the Sky,
For put them side by side,
The one the other will contain,
With ease, and, you beside.

The tension that is evident when symbols point to an oppositional dilemma/conflict; the necessity of this tension for progress via the unconscious; and the presence of suspended animation or hiatus prior to a big breakthrough, made me realize the

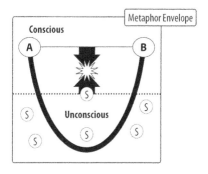

Figure 7.4: Energy streams down to the unconscious mind to activate the symbol(s)

similarities with Jung's work. Going beyond the more limiting scope of Freud's theory, Jung made significant innovations with regard to the functioning of the human psyche. These include, but are not limited to the collective unconscious and the archetypes. An understanding of these constructs is necessary as I am inclined to believe that what happens during the animation process within the metaphor envelope transcends the conscious actions of the ego,[9] including personal memories, logic and insight (the latter is conceived to be the *effect* of the animation process, rather than its cause).

In order to understand the process of working with opposites within the metaphor envelope and the feelings that you are going through, I thought it worthwhile to clarify Jung's terminology a little. Jung[10] envisaged the presence of a collective unconscious which can be distinguished from the personal unconscious in that it does not depend on personal experience. The contents of the collective unconscious have *never been conscious,* and were therefore not acquired by the individual. They are collective and impersonal. This principle relates to the fundamentals of faith – to believe in something *because* it is not tangible (believing-is-seeing) and cannot be grasped through the currency of ego, which is driven by 'seeing-is-believing' ('proof') and capacities vested solely in the individual. Hence, my earlier point in the introductory chapter that the success of personal transformation through metaphor animation hinges on your belief that dynamics are at work which transcend your conscious capabilities and grasp (something your ego may be decidedly uncomfortable with). These capabilities and insights have never been conscious and are 'delivered' by the symbols as unconscious carriers of 'oxygen for spiritual growth', much like blood hemoglobin carries oxygen for life.

The personal unconscious (a Freudian construct) on the other hand is made up of material that has previously been conscious, but became unconscious through forgetting or being repressed (forced outside awareness). Archetypes (defined as 'first of its kind') are central to the idea of the collective unconscious and are 'pre-existent forms' (Jung, 1959, p. 43). They are like motifs or templates that give shape to psychic contents once they hit consciousness. As potentialities they are, however, also dependent on becoming conscious and therefore tangible. It appears that archetypes are involved in:

- shaping new symbols at the level of the collective unconscious and these symbols, once conscious, bolster the animation process, thereby resulting in a breakthrough/ transformation; and/or
- the symbols interact with each other at the level of the collective unconscious through involvement of the archetypes and start to lay the foundation for reconciliation of opposites. Once conscious, they result in you (as the animator/beneficiary) recognizing new relationships and associations between existing symbols which then results in a breakthrough/transformation.

The tension arising from the dilemma of opposing forces somehow 'ignites' the above processes. Jung (1969) confirms that the energy of the archetypes is not sufficient to rise into consciousness and that a quantum of energy flowing into the unconscious from the conscious is necessary. Given that the metaphor envelope is a contained space, the energy created by the suspended animation of the poles is directed downwards and the archetypes (being energized by/attracted to it) move upwards to receive it. Like someone said to me, 'Pressure makes diamonds.' In the figure above, this point of contact is denoted by the spark which opens a conduit for the symbol(s) to move upward into consciousness, like a birth canal. Here the symbols are given shape and are contextualized in the metaphor envelope and the state of play relating to the animation process. The symbols which emerge through the tension created by the oppositional dilemma are now used to resolve it. Jung (1969) clarifies that a psychological mechanism that *transforms energy is a symbol*. He adds (1972)[11] that the archetypes from whence symbols emerge are 'an unconscious content that is altered by becoming conscious and being perceived, and takes its color from the individual consciousness in which it happens to appear'. As products of the archetypes and autonomous, the symbols need to be engaged with in a *dialogue*, which is exactly what the metaphor animation process seeks to achieve. The energy created through the oppositional dilemma is like a furnace which is used to shape the basic tools of transformation (symbols), which can then be further 'customized' by the ego to serve their purpose within the metaphor envelope which is highly personal. It is much like a waterwheel that, by scooping the water from a stream, 'borrows' the 'will' of the water, which can then be translated into a millstone to grind corn. One could say that the whole process is imbibed with the spirit of the water which is made manifest.

The synthesis of opposites could also be explained from the perspective of quantum physics, where the observer plays a key role in how something manifests, i.e. as a wave[12] *or* as a particle.

The conscious mind definitely serves as an observer of mental content, thereby altering *it* and with that, *itself*. Why is that? According to Jeffrey Schwartz and others, the brain operates according to the rules of quantum mechanics [by way of atoms and subatomic particles that constitute it (e.g. ions and neuro-transmitters)]. Therefore, if the brain is part of the quantum system, it too is changed by the observations it makes. This happens the *moment the observer becomes consciously aware of the new knowledge gained*. This is seen as an explanation as to the cleavage of 'both/and's (unconscious mind) into 'either/or's (observed by the conscious mind). The unconscious (defined as mental content outside immediate awareness) is one where apparent opposites can 'co-exist' quite comfortably, i.e. as *both* a wave *and* a particle. This is referred to as indeterminacy – you can't classify something before it is measured. In psychological terms one could speak of *possibilities* (unconscious; can't be measured), which cease to be so when they become *actuality* (grasped consciously; measurable). Something is gained (actual) and something is lost (the 'balance' of possibility), which simply 'passes the conscious mind by' and remains a 'wave' and 'particle' at the same time. Einstein said it well: 'It is the theory that decides what can be observed.' What we observe consciously is always driven by some sort of theory of what is true. It is this theory which results in self-imposed limitations, something that working with the RGT metaphor overcomes by opening the door wide for possibility to emerge. The symbols as transformational resources are special as they, by definition, contain something hidden and tacit – a sea of possibilities. As images that foster your transformation, they outweigh what comes 'in' through your senses from the outside world.

Just visualize a caterpillar inside the chrysalis: it becomes completely liquid prior to transforming itself into a butterfly. The oppositional dilemmas melt away in the unconscious and coalesce just to emerge in a new form, including all the potential of the 'caterpillar' but superseding it. One could visualize symbols that have not been fully animated as standing with their upper 'bodies' above the surface of the water (conscious: actual), with the rest of their bodies still submerged beneath the surface (unconscious: potential). This part is yet to be panned, like a gold miner would do in a creek, carefully distilling out the gold and letting the clutter wash away. The whole creek is full of potential. Special as they are, when resource symbols strike the conscious mind, their meaning and insight provides for healing of the 'either/or's that the conscious mind had created previously.

The ego is a mere onlooker and facilitator within the envelope, as the resolution which is emerging is beyond its purview and grasp (unconscious). However, the ego, being rooted in the unconscious, does benefit. It is strengthened and less alienated from the Self as a psychic totality and source of healing. This manifests as the feeling commensurate with achieving a breakthrough and the melting away of the tension which first accompanied the ego's fruitless attempts to work out conflicts and dilemmas using reason. Pre-animation/transformation, the ego may have been rigid and inflexible like lead, whereas post-animation it would have shed this cumbersome baggage and become light but strong, like honeycomb structures.[13]

Remember: Just because you can't see the stars in daylight doesn't mean they are not always there, shining brightly. It is simply because the sun is too bright. You need to take a dimmer switch to it to be struck by the starlight. Think of the sun as your ego; the symbols in your transformative metaphor as the stars.

More on the Metaphor Envelope as a Vessel for Change

From the word go, metaphors have always struck me as being: (1) *compact* in their portrayal of a problem or potential solution scenario; and (2) *well-contained*, much like a vessel. Hence, the idea of a *metaphor envelope* came up as a reflection of mental workspace or rather playspace, which animation is supposed to be all about. Think of it as a Symbol Sketch Pad (SSP). Play is a process involving fantasy, intuition and imagination as well as the creation of more than is physically present; a sort of augmentation process.

It was only later (during the time that I wrote this chapter), whilst trawling through Jung's books, that I realized that the notion of an envelope could have more meaning (from a transpersonal perspective) than I initially thought. In fact, Jung was the furthest from my mind when I started thinking about the idea of a text on metaphor animation as a facilitative aid for problem-solving, change or transformation. I was thinking more in the direction of systems theory and Neuro Linguistic Programming, with its focus on:

- the *structure* of experience: 'how' we put our experiences 'together' – what experiential 'scaffolds' we use, rather than;
- 'what', which kicks into gear the rational (rationalizing) mind, distortions, patchy memories and ego with its idiosyncrasies and limited perspective – sometimes offering little resolution.

Hence, I was a little surprised when Jung's work reflected so much resonance with the idea of a metaphor envelope and the process of animation. Two things in particular caught my attention which emphasize the importance of a facilitative environment/receptacle for change (which itself is subject to change) – a place where unconscious energy[14] can be converted and objectified through symbols and the work of transformation can become manifest.

The metaphor envelope: focal point for the unconscious

Jung mentions the 'bridal bed in the field' whereby a farmer has intercourse with his wife in the field with the objective of making the earth fruitful. In so doing, an analogy is established – an association between instinctual energy and the field, with cultivation acquiring the meaning and value of a sexual act. Most importantly, this results in a strong and permanent link: attraction and commitment by the farmer to the field as a focal point for growth (this is obviously beneficial for fertility). This idea of a link being formed that is so strong as to transform both the field *and* the farmer brings other examples of fields to mind. One such field is referred to in *The Field*, a book which was turned into an Oscar-winning film with Richard Harris. After re-reading Jung, I made linkages with something particular from the film, but for the first time grasping it at a deeper level and with reference to the idea of an envelope as a vessel and workspace for change. The film starts with the main actors carrying a load of seaweed across a mountainous region to their field. The main character in the book/film is described as striding 'purposefully to the field'. In a commentary about the film and book,[15] Cheryl Herr notes, 'seaweed-toting, rock-breaking and crevice searching[16] all contribute to the production of arable land through human agency. Father, son and soil form a single ensemble of production' (p.58). The enclosed field as a focal point that is invested with the potential to bring forth the fruits of one's labor echoes the function of the metaphor envelope.

By creating a RGT metaphor envelope, the unconscious 'creates' a field and makes it fruitful by placing initial symbols,[17] which are imitations[18] of its desires as reflected in the metaphor (as object of libido), in it. These symbols become objects of expectation and great interest much like a treasure, once buried, can form a lifelong attraction and purpose for the person who buried it, until it is unearthed and its contents put to use. The dynamic behind the metaphor envelope is similar: by coming up with the RGT metaphor, the unconscious creates for itself a workspace (like the fruitful field). It forms a strong bond, thus creating a conduit to receive the unconscious mind's symbols which can be further animated to fully unfold and solidify their resourceful functions. Much like a treasure it has a high value and stimulates the imagination, even fantasy, resulting in focus and commitment.

Metaphor animation as a labor of love

Symbols need to be enticed to 'leave' the unconscious and core archetypes from which they arise, much like a rabbit must be tempted to leave its haunt with a carrot. Having lovingly created its 'flowerbed', 'fenced' it (the RGT metaphor envelope), and put some icons (symbols) in it, the unconscious made an initial 'investment' and with that created a bond and formed a commitment. The icons are contained in the metaphor that was translated from the negative to the positive (see Chapter 5) but need to be developed further, whereas others need to be elicited. The animation process plays a critical role in this regard as it helps to 'pull' the symbols toward consciousness. The symbols as messengers from the unconscious archetypes are numinous. By virtue of having a specific energy, they display an affinity for the contents of your conscious mind, much like a water droplet will cling to a finger. As ideas about ideas, the symbols require conscious ideas to make them tangible and able to be reflected upon by the 'animator' (you). This further matures them and increases their functionality and impact. This helps to reveal their inherent characteristics as resources, offering a new perspective on an existing predicament(s) during the journey to attain the RGT metaphor scenario. As this happens, you will be struck by a sudden enlightenment and revelation (moment of clarity) or a more subtle but equally powerful intuition.[19] The animation process is a bit like a midwife assisting in a birth – the baby contains all the potential but has to be pulled toward the light and hit on the bum to inhale air and become fully able to function outside the womb. Symbols always contain something tacit and are yet to be unearthed (which is what the animation process is all about). The animation process serves to turn potentiality (locked up in the symbols) into actuality, when you become aware of their role in progressively directing you to the resolution or outcome(s) reflected in the positive or RGT metaphor.

The animation process is a playful way to entice symbols and – once they are conscious – engage with them. It is a process that ensures ongoing fascination as it becomes apparent that more symbols reveal their nature and the incredibly invigorating or novel perspectives they provide. Be prepared for this to fire up your imagination to engage further with the symbols, leading to new discoveries and keeping you inspired, involved and hungry for more. This is indicative of the notion that the metaphor envelope becomes an object of expectation (like the field for the farmer) which is then fueled to reveal more through actual committed engagement. All the while, you are fostering a working relationship between the symbols and your psyche. The Self as the psychic totality plays a key role in organizing this activity. As previously discussed, the ego (what you are conscious of at any given time) is merely a servant – clay in the hands of the Self. By 'subjecting' itself to the hands of the creator during the animation process it aids transformation, but more importantly is transformed *by it*. Remember, though, that the conscious mind does not create symbols – at best it unpacks them and polishes them up to the highest level of sheen. The change you desire is reflected in them.

The animation process is probably like fervently rubbing a magic lamp so that the genie may appear. Jung (1969) contends that the symbol has to offer some sort of gradient and channel, which is steeper than ordinary run-off (if we were to compare libido to a river). This will transform the libido into a purposeful symbol that is recognized as such by you as the animator. (Visualize molten gold being poured into a form; a gas flame directed and focused through a nozzle). Animation therefore reinforces symbol formation. It facilitates a process whereby symbols, as converted energy, 'tilt' toward the conscious mind, rather than tilting backward, and dipping into the sea of fuzzy unconscious energy, where they remain intangible and uncon- structive in terms of achieving change. Because the currency of the unconscious differs, the symbols are necessary to turn poten- tiality into actuality.

The link between the unconscious and conscious therefore is not direct, and an intermittent step of 'currency conversion' and bridge-building across the divide is necessary. This step is the symbol formation. 'The Self is virtually a transcendental concept; it cannot be known directly by the ego, but only indirectly through symbol, dream and myth.'[20] The thick arrow in the figure below does not point directly from unconscious to the conscious mind but dips to indicate the domain of transfor- mation, much like the butterfly transforms via a cocoon. This domain is where symbols are articulated and once you become conscious of them, they become manifest. As the figure below shows (by example), the symbols are like little 'pies' with slices missing. The 'slices' that are 'missing' have 'graduated' to the conscious mind and started to populate the metaphor envelope, creating the basis for new associations. However, in line with their definition (*synbolon*: 'thrown together'), symbols always retain a hidden or tacit aspect – something that is being signified. These are the aspects that have not yet become conscious. They are linked to the parts of symbols which are already conscious. They are entangled to ensure that a bridge, like a 'star-gate', exists to enable the progressive 'movement' of the 'residual' meaning and purpose of the symbol to consciousness. The meaning of the symbols, whilst distributed (between conscious and unconscious mind, respectively), remains inseparable – i.e. that a 'bridge' links them to convey the meaning coherently and definitively. (This is depicted by the dotted circle, which alludes to the ultimate shift of the total meaning of the symbol(s) into conscious awareness).

It is important to note that this bridge does not merely exist abstractly in the metaphor envelope, but *is the real you*. The symbols are part of you, even if at first you may not recognize their meaning. As the meaning emerges due to the animation process, you will experience the insight and change at a subjective level in the form of very tangible and real change. This change will be as relieving as it is enlightening, showing once again that irreconcilable differences or polarities exist only insofar as the ego is convinced that they cannot be resolved. Hence it is not the problems that cannot be resolved – it is the ego's obstinacy and grandiosity that stands in the way of achieving resolution. The ego is not willing or able to grasp a reality (the essence of the 'Self') (Jung) beyond the scope of its own conscious thoughts and perceived abilities. This is the most regrettable form of ignorance that one can imagine, as it makes some believe that their problems are unsolvable or wishes unattainable, resulting in hopelessness, anxiety or depression.

The animation process plays a key role in:

- manifesting the symbols for you in visible form; and then
- 'shuttling' the meaning of the symbols between the unconscious and unconscious mind (note: the symbols themselves appear to you consciously as comprehensive or definitive, but their full *meaning* is not yet clear). In a way, the symbols are themselves mini envelopes or vessels that are transported into conscious awareness, their meaning then becoming manifest. The metaphor envelope serves like a hidden passageway to direct and focus that which the unconscious mind seeks to project

upward into consciousness.

Once the full meaning of the symbols is known to you as the animator/beneficiary, they have again become 'whole'; their meaning chunks have coalesced. With that, they cease to be symbols as they no longer have tacit and unexplored dimensions (simultaneously 'wave' and 'particle'). The symbols are therefore no longer purveyors of possibility (through interaction with the conscious mind through our senses, the wave function has collapsed into actuality). Once they have served their purpose, symbols become like fireflies that are no longer visible at the break of dawn (in this case, the dawn of inspiration). Or they become like a cocoon from which the butterfly has freed itself, its transformation role being complete. By this time, the symbols would have helped you with remedial changes, the generation of new approaches or transformation, all of which will manifest beyond the metaphor envelope and translate into your lived experiences.

It is important to remember that symbols are unlikely to exist independent of the meaning *you* attach to them. Whilst it is possible that the symbols which emerge in the metaphor envelope have universal or fixed meanings, this is not really important. It is important that they are messengers of the unconscious and the archetypes. They contain many potential meanings. What matters is what they mean to *you*. They are more important as *processes* than what shape or form they take or what they are called (their names are really arbitrary labels). Remember this: things that seem impossible for your reasoning mind are possible within the metaphor envelope. The challenge is sweet surrender.

My experience with clients has shown that the process of symbol formation through animation continues for days and even weeks, as the energy from the unconscious is transformed into fruitful conduits and toward a positive, conscious outcome.

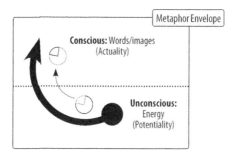

Figure 7.5: Symbol formation through the animation process

Think of this as potentiation. This outcome is the achievement of the RGT metaphor and the resolution, through symbols, of polarities that may stand in its way. The process of animation seems to continue more or less automatically (unconsciously), with symbols popping up spontaneously and often quite unexpectedly as long as you remain receptive. They will offer new orientations towards certain conflicts or impasses, ranging from the tiniest of puzzle pieces in the metaphor envelope to quite dramatic shifts and an overhaul within the current arrangement of symbols. Whatever happens, the results are more often than not enlightening – offering new stepping stones or new landscapes. In the words of Jung: 'much is needed to divert the libido from its natural riverbed of everyday habit into some unaccustomed activity' (p.52). Metaphor animation is one such unaccustomed activity. It is a journey which is quite unfamiliar, with new unknown mental 'lands' emerging around every corner. Its final outcome is hard to imagine, were it not for the pointers or scenario included in the RGT metaphor.

Example of animating the RGT metaphor further

Having clarified what happens in the case of oppositional dilemmas and why, we can go back to the example of 'My life is (like) plain sailing' and expand on this RGT metaphor by applying the additional and more incisive animation questions set out in the previous chapter. (Refer to the table in Chapter 6.) First, the essence of the oppositional dilemma as experienced by the person (metaphor beneficiary) is going to be unpacked and clarified. If you look at the table you would have noted the following:

Oppositional dilemma: External
'Others are the wind in my sails, but they must also get what they want.' This is an extended secondary metaphor[21] that was created as a result of the animation process. The donor domain symbol ('wind') 'revealed' its purpose to the metaphor beneficiary, namely that meaningful others are recognized as a resource. However, the precondition attached to this ('but they must also get what they want') manifested as an oppositional dilemma, i.e. 'If they get what they want, I may not get what I want', and vice versa. This created an obstacle and gave rise to a typical 'between a rock and a hard place' impasse.

Oppositional dilemma: Internal
The internal oppositional dilemma related to the person being in 'two minds', with one 'part' wanting to 'up and plain sail' (creating fear), whereas the other wants to stay put (creating safety but frustration). One could think of this as ambition (drive) vs. inhibition.

Task: Further animation to resolve oppositional dilemmas
The above oppositional dilemmas were explored by further animating the symbols. It provides further refined techniques by way of example that you may not have thought of before to:

- unlock some of the symbols that may not have availed their meaning; and
- reveal further symbols; relationships between symbols; and/or relationships between the symbols and the RGT

metaphor/envelope as a whole.

MAIN TASK: USE THE TECHNIQUES IN THE EXAMPLE BELOW TO REFINE YOUR OWN ANIMATION PROCESS UNDER STEP 3 (CHAPTER 6)

i. Ocean

In the case of the ocean symbol, I asked the person:

- about their vantage point, i.e. from where they were looking at the ocean. This revealed that they were looking at it from the seashore within the harbor. This reflected a calm, deep blue ocean. A change of vantage point to beyond the harbor and to deep waters revealed towering, rolling waves and brought about a change in color from bright blue to dark grey/black.
- the typology question, 'What *type* of an ocean does this appear to be?' This yielded, 'It is ominous and threatening. It presents an obstacle, even though it is also a necessity – being the medium and linkage between origin and destination. One has to endure it. Once you have passed the halfway mark, you are closer to your destination than your place of origin.' To a follow-up typology question, 'What type of a destination does this appear to be?' he replied, 'Vague and shrouded in the mist, but that's OK – it heightens the sense of adventure. After all, in life, we don't always need to know where we are going to and how this may look; otherwise everything would become predictable and there would be no challenges.'
- the time-line question, 'What happens, going forward, and how does this change things?' This yielded the following response: 'After the rough patch comes a

smooth patch – bad weather does not last forever.' This brought about a significant shift in that something funda-mental (ocean as 'freedom and prison cell') changed into *something situational/short-term, time-bound and therefore manageable.*

ii. Portholes

Their purpose and intent was unclear for the person that generated the RGT metaphor. We tried the following approaches:

- ZOOMING in closer;
- LOOKING at the portholes through his own eyes (associated) (situated 'in/on the boat');
- MOVING time from day-time to night-time,
  - 'switching on the light in the boat';
  - 'switching off the light in the boat';[22] and
- ASKING about the symbol's (portholes') intent.

With an extreme 'zoom-in', the person became aware of his own reflection in the portholes. It became clear what this reflection meant when we asked the metaphor to reveal its purpose. The symbol sought to convey the notion of 'self-knowledge', which requires self-reflection. It also became clear that this meaning had an impact on another symbols, namely 'ocean' and the associated insight (see above).

iii. Anchor

The anchor as a dualistic resource ensures safety but simulta-neously also prevents achievement of the remedial, gener-ative or transformative objective reflected by the metaphor. We used the following additional animating questions to resolve both extremes of the oppositional dilemma (safety vs. immobility).

- diminishing the features/sub-sensory qualities of the anchor, in this case, its size. Turning the anchor into a tiny toy anchor would allow it to be dragged by the boat, seemingly resolving the moving/staying dilemma. However, this proved to be counter-productive due to the dual nature of its function, namely securing and holding back. It became apparent that other conditions had to be met. In fact, accentuating the features of the anchor, by making it heavy so that it could secure the boat well, was perceived as highly desirable until such time as further insight was forthcoming.

- conditions or requirements for change: it was clear from the above (first bullet) that the anchor was fulfilling a legitimate role and would resist meta-sensory animation[23] attempts. Further animation was clearly required to unlock further meaning and/or to elicit further symbols.

Oppositional dilemma: External

The external dilemma was clarified as follows by way of a sequence of events, which starts with 'Lift anchor' and 'Don't lift anchor' scenarios (see figures below). Both of these choices are interrelated and end where they started ('the more things change, the more they stay the same'). In the scenario, 'Lift anchor', there appears to be a way out ('I get what I want'), but only temporarily. When guilt starts to emerge, the person is discouraged from plain sailing, due to the perceived adverse impact on others. For a short while, 'not lifting the anchor' seems to be a desirable option, but running this course (see figure to the right) also creates a problem. Subsequently, anger results (about feeling guilty; and not achieving the objective/need/desire). This intensifies the focus on the opposi-tional dilemma for which there appears to be no resolution, but also keeps the objective (wanting to plain sail) alive. This is positive, as the *concurrent* awareness of the apparent non-viability of *both polarities* (and resulting hiatus) is what will activate the symbols that have the power to transcend the problems at hand and reconcile them. The energized archetype that avails itself through the transformative symbols corresponds with the dilemma at hand and is therefore able to attach itself (like the 'hundreds and thousands') to the conscious mind in the form of recognizable images.

In the case of 'Don't lift anchor', the 'solution' (staying put) results in others getting what they want, which initially also seems to be an option. This is until resentfulness emerges, which results in the shadow emotion of guilt (about being resentful towards others) and then anger, which shifts the focus to the other option, i.e. wanting to 'lift the anchor'. However, as the above analysis shows, this also ends up where it started.

In both instances there appears to be no real resolution. It is important to note that in both instances, emotions played an important role. Specifically, 'shadow emotions' resulted in the vicious cycle. Shadow emotions refer to those emotions which 'pop up' almost immediately, 'behind' an initial emotion, and influence the subjective emotional state and how one thinks about things and acts on them. Have you ever been angry at someone (with or without them knowing) and suddenly felt a burst of guilt about feeling angry, perhaps after you looked at the person more empathically? It is the shadow emotion(s) which can have a tempering (or intensifying) effect on the initial one(s). Most importantly, the shadow emotions that arise as one goes through the progression of events play a key role in the outcomes on both sides of the pole (decision not to plain sail; pressure to plain sail; decision to plain sail; pressure not to plain sail). You should therefore not avoid the emotions or view them as undesirable. They are critical as they:

- attest to the fact that there is a gap between where you are (as reflected in the negative metaphor) and where you want to be (as reflected in the RGT metaphor) (this is the feeling of being 'out of kilter'); and
- help you (as a form of generative energy) to stay focused on, and motivated to achieve the desired change (the scenario reflected in the RGT metaphor).

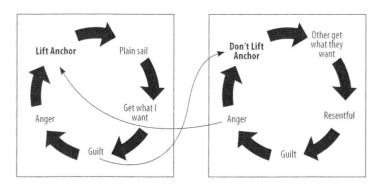

Figure 7.6: Oppositional dilemma: External

Oppositional dilemma: Internal

The internal dilemma was clarified as follows:

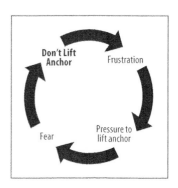 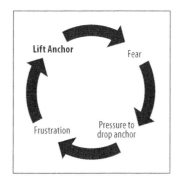

Figure 7.7: Oppositional dilemma: Internal

The above is a clear self-perpetuating cycle with no satis-factory outcome. Lifting the anchor and not lifting the anchor both produce emotions and outcomes that are unproductive and undesirable. Whereas frustration provides impetus to 'plain sail', the ensuing fear puts paid to this plan (but already creates a comfort zone due to perpetuation of the status quo). The boat stays moored because there are symbols which have not yet emerged to aid in the resolution of the dilemma by transcending the ostensibly (only for the ego, that is) irresolvable oppositional dilemma.

MAIN TASK:
DRAW YOUR OWN OPPOSITIONAL DILEMMAS (INTERNAL/EXTERNAL), USING THE ABOVE FIGURES AS AN EXAMPLE. USE YOUR DRAWING AS A BASIS TO FURTHER ANIMATE THE RGT METAPHOR TO OVERCOME THE POLARITIES AND TO VALIDATE THEIR RESOLUTION.

The symbols are necessary to prevent the intense emotions becoming chronic due to the oscillation between unviable options/poles with their self-perpetuating cycles. The symbols prevent emotional entropy[24] which can lead to your inability or unwillingness to make changes (depression/learned helplessness). The primary role of the self-perpetuating cycles in the case of both the internal and external dilemmas is to ensure that change does not happen too rapidly. This is achieved through the cycles reflecting both progression and regression (back to the oppositional dilemma) until a more viable approach has been found (through the resources offered by the symbols). This viable approach is a transformation in the structure of what you know, resulting in deeper insights and resourcefulness.

Oscillating between the two polarities and the self-perpetuating cycles within them, therefore, is a bit like a jet plane in a holding pattern over an airport: it makes progress when it flies toward the airport and lack of progress when it flies away from it. Once it has a go-ahead from the tower (the resolution), it knows which runway to touch down on. Similarly, once the animation process has yielded all the resource symbols, transcendence of the oppositional dilemma can be achieved and with that the intense negative emotions abate too. Positive/affirming emotions take their place. This shows that the gap between where you were and where you want to be (RGT metaphor) has been narrowed and/or eliminated.

The following approach was used:

- review of the symbols that are already available but not fully explored (refer to Table 6.1 in Chapter 6 above). Here the focus fell on the boat. The person was asked how they represented the boat to themselves. It turned out that the boat was viewed from a *disassociated* perspective and at a distance; and

- exploration of additional symbols that may transcend the oppositional dilemma through a process of reconciliation at a more profound and holistic level.

i. Secondary animation questions

- Stepping into the envelope and onto the boat as symbol; and

- Using a combination of putting himself *in* the picture (in this case getting onto the 'boat' symbol) and looking *into* it yielded further breakthroughs to resolve the oppositional dilemma of staying [(not 'plain sailing') (frustration) and going (plain sailing) (fear)]. The person recognized supplies in the boat, which brought the insight (through a secondary metaphor) that being 'well equipped' would attenuate some of the fear of tackling the ocean (plain sailing). It also made him realize that it is better to 'cast one's bread on the water' and learn by commission (sailing: fear) rather than omission (not sailing: frustration/safety). Doing something (commission) results in tangible feedback from which we can learn and adjust our approaches and with that increase our chances of success.

Being on the boat also availed the 'wind turbine' symbol. In response to the typology question, 'What type of wind turbine might this be?' the person responded as follows: 'The wind turbine is fixed to the boat, higher up, to catch the wind. It is used to charge the batteries. For me it means that as long as I am moving (plain sailing) I am actually storing energy for when the wind dies down. My navigation instruments (compass), lights and motor will still work. I would not have to call for assistance, but could simply wait out the hiatus and then move along, or use the motor. I see it as a form of preparing for and securing the future. If I had stayed in the harbor, I would have been safe but can also not achieve any growth. For this to happen, the boat must actually be moving.'

Leaning over the edge of the boat and looking into the water evoked the notions of a treasure on the sea floor, and specifically that of coins. The resource symbol typology question, 'What type of symbols might these be?' revealed 'trick coins' with two heads, rather than heads and tails. The question, 'What might the purpose be of these two-headed coins?' yielded the following responses (in terms of the external dilemma):

- 'life needn't be "either/or"'; and
- 'life needn't be comprised of events in sequence, i.e. that the one process (something negative) has to take its course

prior to another (something positive) being able to start.'

'The double-headed coin brought the realization to me that others can get what they want whilst I get what I want. The one does not have to depend on the other first coming to fruition.' This precondition clearly only existed at the level of the ego. The animation process was able to resolve the matter at a higher level, thus 'evaporating' the obstacle to plain sailing. Union between the ego and Self within the metaphor envelope therefore resulted in union in the relational world. Previously, splits in the psyche resulted in divisions in the world and with others.

ii. Summary: creating the total picture

The figure (influence diagram) below serves as a holistic summary of what has already been achieved. When you do your animation, it will become evident that grouping the symbols, based on their characteristics and how they interrelate, will unlock further insights that can be reconciliatory and transcend what the ego sees as insurmountable. The arrows show cause-and-effect relationships, i.e. how symbols contribute to certain outcomes as reflected in the RGT. The dotted line shows symbols that are similar in their purpose or function even though their form or characteristics differ. The figure below shows that the 'two-headed coin', 'supplies in boat', and to a lesser extent the 'wind turbine' are tipping-point resources. They nudged the events in the metaphor toward irrevocable and fundamental (holistic) change, which was subjectively experienced as such by the metaphor beneficiary. Eventually, the anchor was lifted and plain sailing became possible without the usual oppositional dilemmas (and unbearable and unproductive emotional tension) manifesting.

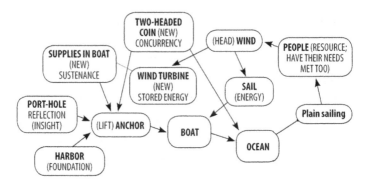

Figure 7.8: Influence diagram: the fruits of RGT metaphor animation

Some Comments on the Change and Transformation Process

One can't help but notice how the process of growth and transformation in this person is reflected in a change in the symbols and their derived meaning:

i.   In the beginning, an oppositional conflict appears between individual drives/ambitions and those of meaningful others. This attests to a lack of autonomy and a conflict between pleasing (outwardly directed ego through the persona (mask)) vs. asserting/true independence and authenticity (inwardly directed ego; toward the Self). Meaningful others could be seen as proxies for parents and notably lack of proper separation from them. During this time, the symbols are matriarchal (the weak ego identifying with the anima[25]) and reflect a need for security and nurturing (ocean; harbor). The emotions are immature and include fear; anger; resentfulness and frustration.

ii.   As the animation process starts to reveal more symbols and their meaning becomes clear too, the ego is rebalanced against the Self. There is shift from 'either/or' to a union (double-headed coin) of what previously were opposites. The symbols are less matriarchal (harbor; water) and become more patriarchal (sky; air/wind).[26] The supplies in the boat are a sign of preparation; logic and foresight for the life journey. The boat 'lifts' the person out of the matriarchal 'ocean' (lifting of the mind threshold); the wind propels him along and gives him mobility, autonomy and direction (but also exhilaration and invigoration: hair blown back by the wind). The wind turbine ensures his independence, as it keeps navigation instruments, lights and the motor going. The porthole reflections ensure self-insight and with that an ability to recognize and heed personal limitations (true masculinity). The metaphorical 'harbor' (the need for mother's nurturing) disappears in the distance. These are all indications of a strengthened ego, independence, growth, transformation and the emergence of true masculinity, but always in balance with the matriarchate. The boat remains in touch with and turned toward the ocean but a healthy boundary now exists. The ocean no longer threatens or limits, but empowers. The ego is turned toward the anima and derives strength from it rather than being engulfed by it. The ego is, however, also turned toward the world and its challenges. Jung would refer to this as a balance between the feminine and masculine energies.

Remember: The 'stars' in the form of symbols were able to enlighten the person to whom the example above applies, because his ego ('sun') adopted its required place of humility and thereby allowed itself to grow, transform and be strengthened from the inside (Self).

Summary

✓ The chapter provided greater clarity on oppositional dilemmas, which can be internal (such as when you have difficulty 'making up your mind'), or external. The latter can include having to face two equally desirable or undesirable options ('a rock and a hard place'). It is often not the choices or conflicts themselves but their perceived *consequences* which bring about unwanted emotions that individuals seek to avoid. Going with *either* option usually only brings temporary 'joy' until stuck points and negative emotions re-appear. However, going with *neither* is usually perceived as a cop-out as it prevents growth and rising up to challenges posed, as life progresses. The above can take the form of perpetuating cycles, like being in an eternal mental 'holding pattern'. This is where the resource symbols come in: they transcend the oppositional dilemmas by bringing about resolutions at another level, thereby highlighting a way forward that is acceptable and emotionally neutral (as far as negative emotions are concerned); and emotionally exciting (as far as positive emotions are concerned).

✓ Oppositional dilemmas, despite creating emotional strain, are the very life-blood of the animation process which is aimed at eliciting symbols that will bring about reconciliation of polarities and attain the scenario spelled out in the RGT metaphor. The *way* that you look at a problem changes, and with that the problem ceases to exist or is accepted (as you change).

✓ As long as only one polarity is conscious at any given time and there exists a flexible alternation (turn-taking of poles between conscious and unconscious mind), the situation does not come to a head. It is only when the animation process forces matters to a tipping point that you would become consciously aware of oppositional dilemmas.

✓ Becoming consciously aware of polarities (internal and/or external) *simultaneously* creates a state of *suspended animation* or hiatus. The metaphor animation process simply stalls and emotional tension remains. This energy is released and directed into the unconscious where it releases resource symbols.

✓ The energy is contained (safe and manageable) in the metaphor envelope and needs to be allowed to do its work (elicit symbols), as opposed to you directing it into the environment or against others. This can be tempting due to the tension experienced, which can easily be displaced onto the environment. Valuable energy required for change is then lost. Your ego would therefore have to keep its propensity to (re)act in abeyance, accepting that a bigger picture [unfathomable by the conscious mind (and facilitated by active engagement in animation)], is at work.

✓ The symbols which arise are able to reconcile any opposi-tional dilemmas which you have become aware of during the metaphor animation process.

✓ The chapter enabled you to explore relationships among symbols by drawing them and indicating which symbols influence or are influenced by others, and which associa-tions they evoke.

ENDNOTES

1 Senge (1990). The Fifth Discipline.

2 Bradshaw, 1988.

3 The emotional intensity around reverting back to baseline, however, may increase with every self-perpetuating 'round', resulting in and intensifying the despondency and hopelessness.

4 Look out for the next book in this series which revolves around using RGT metaphor to transform relationships.

5   Because both poles are appealing or not appealing or because we can't make up our mind (internal oppositional dilemma (in 'two minds'), we do tend to expend significant mental resources considering the 'options' exhaustively in turn, in the hope of being able to find resolution.

6   Bearing in mind that some people tend to channel this energy into the environment through typical ego-defenses, including displacing the tension onto others or inanimate objects (primary defenses), or through sublimation, e.g. channeling it into socially laudable pursuits such as sports; academic achievements etc. Metaphor animation offers a mental field where this energy can be converted productively to the benefit of personal growth.

7   Refer also to the books by Weinrib and Turner on Sandplay Therapy for further clarity.

8   According to Freud's theory, the ego mediates between social demands, norms and values as embodied by the Superego and the unconscious drives, using the reality principle. The unconscious drives have to subsume themselves to 'reality'. The ongoing mediation process results in tensions, which are released in the form of so-called ego-defenses which are projected onto the outside world and people.

9   The ego is what you are aware of at any given time and can subjectively identify as 'you'. It is a mere enclave within your total psychic landscape but likes to claim achievements as being due to its sole effort and ability. Failures are disowned. According to Jung, however, the Self is the subject of the total psyche and forms an organizing force, including the 'rightsizing' or rebalancing of the ego, when the latter becomes too grandiose; our pursuits too one-sided. It does so by instituting a balancing force- a form of compensation. Who has not experienced the dichotomies in personal experience (without suffering from bipolar

disorder), whereby the highest highs are usually followed by an equivalent low (and *vice versa*)? The one somehow cannot exist without the other, much like day cannot be grasped without knowledge of its counter-position, being night.

10 Jung, 1959.

11 Editor's note, p.4.

12 Wave and particle' are merely used as an example from quantum physics to demonstrate that for the unconscious mind the 'world is your oyster', and that many realities exist. It is the conscious mind (observation) which prunes these 'realities' into a select few. As Schwartz (2002) notes, "the mind of the observer helps choose which of an uncountable number of possible realities comes into being in the form of observations" (p.273) [(the observations it makes changes it too - the moment the observer becomes aware of the new knowledge gained (through the observation)].

13 Really strong structures are flexible and light. This is why honeycomb designs make up aircraft wings. They are light enough to allow for flight, but strong and flexible enough to prevent disintegration in hostile environments. The same 'mix' is necessary for success at life and living.

14 Jung speaks of the 'canalisation of libido' (energy), whereby psychic intensities or values are transferred from one content to another, like water being boiled, turned into steam and used to drive a turbine for electricity generation. Symbols are therefore 'libido analogues', since they give equivalent expression to the libido, by channeling it into a different, productive and palpable form.

15 'Sheridan and *The Field*'.

16 The reference to fertility cannot help but strike one.

17 This is what the envelope contains, pre-animation.

18 This is much like a turbine 'imitating' the flow of water

(original object of instinct), thereby being able to put it to good use.

19 According to Jung, archetypes are numinous (mystical; spiritual; magical), hence their power to create insights that can supersede apparent polarities, which appear irreconcilable at the level of the ego.

20 Tacey, 2006, p.48.

21 Often, symbols also arise cloaked as a 'secondary metaphor', thus offering resolution in this manner. Secondary metaphor therefore need not be negative or point to a problem. Often, secondary metaphor is more powerful than individual symbols. (Secondary metaphor is defined as metaphor within metaphor, i.e. when the animation process reveals additional metaphors. These can also be unpacked using the same animation questions, but can, under certain circumstances, reveal their generative, remedial or transformative function right away.)

22 Switching lights on and off is important as a technique as it reveals very different things, e.g. foreground and background [(including the moon/stars or other sources of 'light' (insight) during a dark night)].

23 This means changing the structure and attributes of the symbol(s), using the animation questions dealing with symbol features.

24 Emotional entropy means disorder or randomness. Emotions take their own course rather than being illuminated and transformed through the metaphor animation process and directed towards a higher, even spiritual, purpose. Emotional entropy means that emotions *have* you; resolving polarities means that *you have the emotions* (control is regained). Raising the mind's threshold toward consciousness ensures this.

25 The anima reflects the 'psychic personification of the feminine principle in men' (Weinrib, 2004. p.206). It serves

as a link to the unconscious – a bridge between ego and Self. According to Jung (1959), the anima is a 'natural archetype that sums up all the statements of the unconscious. Man cannot make it; it is in his moods, reactions, impulses' (p.27). He further states that transformation of the 'personality gives prominence to those traits that are characteristic of the opposite sex. Turned toward the world, the anima is fickle, capricious, moody, uncontrolled and emotional' (Jung, 1972, p.67).

26 The color of air and sky depict spiritual contents as it strikes the conscious mind. The warm colors like red are used for feeling and emotions.

Chapter 8

Summary and Conclusion

This book is about a dialogue between the conscious and unconscious mind. It gives the unconscious mind with its unquantifiable resources a voice to apply these in a constructive fashion, reducing the foothold for neurotic conditions. It allows the ego an opportunity to relinquish its delusional perception of omnipotence (and finally strengthen its sense of belonging and relationship to the Self). By doing so, it allows the symbols to do their restorative and transformative work, which is facilitated by the metaphor animation process. The consequence is a renewed sense of motivation, zest for life and emotional well-being. The process strengthens the ego but this time not to the point of inflation but in a manner that will ensure authenticity, humility and sustainability.

As this book shows, Johnson and Lakoff, who did some seminal work on metaphors, were more than right with their book title *Metaphors We Live By*. Indeed we do. Being top of mind (but firmly rooted in the unconscious), metaphors drive our thoughts, emotions and actions. They are a form of matrix in which our minds dwell. If we don't watch ourselves, they can become self-fulfilling prophesies. However, so can positive metaphors: as we generate metaphors that reflect possibilities and future scenarios *as if they were now*, we can free ourselves from our current problems and constraints. By animating generative metaphors we can wrest control back from the outcomes or determinism that is often spelled out in the negative metaphors we use (or the progression of events in our environments). In so doing, we bring *intelligence to* our generative metaphors (the process of animation) and derive *intelligence from* them.

After reading the book and putting the steps to correct use, you should have experienced change and not mere knowledge; perhaps even felt transformation, having new questions arise, or experienced the remediation of pressing problems. This is because this book does not appeal to or rely on your *conscious mind* with its typical information-processing constrains and its host of ego defenses such as rationalization, denial (which effectively block change and transformation), self-sabotage as well as negative self-talk.

You would have experienced the animation process as being highly innovative and novel, using metaphors (specifically positive or prospective metaphor) as a way of engaging with your aspirations, needs or dreams. The hallmark of this method is that it is in principle *content free,* i.e. issues are dealt with in an abstract domain by engaging with ('animating') symbols contained in the metaphor. You would have noted that there was no need to interpret or reflect on substantive issues relating to life, work, or relationships. In fact, you would have found conscious engagement with the RGT metaphor by way of interpretation as being *counter-productive* given that your conscious mind does not contain the vast resources of the unconscious. The animation process itself, which unlocks unconscious resources (revealed by symbols as its messengers), would have yielded the insight and change you desired.

This should have been achieved effortlessly, drawing on your *active imagination,*[1] *intuition, playfulness and curiosity.* Your only engagement would have been with the *structure or attributes* of the symbols contained in your RGT metaphor.

Post-animation, you should now feel the insights gained as manifesting in your real-life experiences and in the form of ordinary (non-metaphoric) narrative. In other words, change in the metaphor at a symbolic level (through animation) is now manifesting as substantive change at the level of your mind, brain and behavior. This leap between metaphor and your 'real life' would have been due to the RGT metaphor being a particularly rich representation and structurally similar to the organization of *how* and *what* you know. Expect these changes to become sustainable as the mental force you brought to bear (through engaging with and animating your RGT metaphor) alters your brain. As discussed, mental force is conceived of as a *physical force* that acts on your brain as physical 'matter' (which is highly plastic and malleable). Jungian psychology explains how unconscious resources are made conscious through symbols, the resulting insight of which is the fulcrum for the change you can experience.

In summary then, the book revealed the following:

- A NOVEL and highly effective approach to achieve your life, work, relationship or other goals, needs or dreams by engaging with what has been termed the RGT metaphor;
- THE fruitfulness of engaging with metaphors rather than your ordinary thoughts as expressed in day-to-day narrative is based on the fact that your reality (and to a large extent your own thoughts) remain fundamentally unknowable. Rich as they are, metaphors (notably those stated positively) are therefore a brilliant shot at fostering understanding and change at a level much deeper than thoughts themselves would permit. Furthermore, metaphor ordered your thoughts and reflected issues and aspirations in a compact yet definitive manner.
- THE PROCESS of engaging with metaphor is called *animation*. The process of animation serves to elicit and unpack symbols which are unconscious resources aimed at achieving what the positive metaphor embodies (set out therein as a future scenario). The symbols are particularly effective in reconciling seemingly irreconcilable stuck-points and polarities;
- THE METAPHOR animation process is entirely content free.

You engaged with metaphor symbols at the level of their structure and attributes. There was no need to engage with your objectives, needs or aspirations in a substantive, rational manner. In so doing, the infor-mation-processing constraints of your conscious mind were circumvented as were obstacles to change (e.g. self-sabotage; and defense mechanisms such as rational-ization, denial, procrastination, passive-aggressive behavior, etc.). The metaphor animation process drew on your imagination, playfulness and curiosity. How to animate the RGT metaphor was described in detail and clarified using a case study and examples; and

- THE INSIGHTS yielded by the animation process readily translate into change and transformation which manifests in 'real life' (non-symbolic; non-metaphoric). These are enduring changes due to the impact at the level of mind ('software') and brain ('malleable-ware').

Perhaps you have now learned that the RGT metaphor is a *gift*. It may have freed you from stifling thoughts and the limitations of a perceived negative 'here and now' or fear for what the future may hold. It did so by focusing your mind very strongly on *possibility and gating your thoughts and neural pathways away from actuality*. It helped you visualize and project your expecta-tions as a form of prospective 'reality' but also provided the necessary structure and resources to make you attain it. It made your future *now*, as there is no time to wait for it to materialize.

RGT Metaphor: Your wish is its command. My wish as the author is for this book and the method of metaphor animation to really bring you the change you want. I am certainly confident that it can.

I would like to conclude with an excerpt from my favorite and most treasured poem, *Herbsttag* (English translation: 'Autumn Day'[2)] by Rainer Maria Rilke (1875–1926) (my italics).

Lord: it is time.
The summer was *immense*.
Lay your *shadow* on the sundials
and *let loose* the wind in the fields.

Bid the last fruits to be *full*;
give them another two more southerly days,
press them to *ripeness*, and *chase* the last *sweetness* into the
heavy wine.

The above poem is deeply metaphorical and contains exceptionally vivid, sensory and active/animated symbols-in-motion (see my italics). Although one cannot be sure exactly what the author meant to convey, the poem appears to refer to (his?) life stages and specifically the progression from summer, through autumn, to winter (advancing age). It also talks about maturation and opportunity and wresting the last 'sweetness' from the summer of life. Tacey (2006) reminds us that the archetypal figures (the Self is the central archetype) are *processes* rather than objects and never fixed or unchanging, but 'fluid metaphors' (pp.20–21). The Rilke poem reflects such fluidity of the metaphors, which may well mirror the changing psychic processes and perhaps even the transformation, psychic renewal and individuation (fruitful integration of ego and the unconscious mind) of the poet.

ENDNOTES

1   According to Jung (1969), active imagination puts us in a position of advantage as we can make the discovery of the archetype without sinking back into the sphere of our instincts.

2   www.poemhunter.com.

Glossary of Terms

Animation (verb): the transformative power of symbols is tacit, i.e. not immediately apparent. The animation process makes them release their 'payload' and with that their energy which brings about the change you want. In this sense, it is a facilitative process. The ego is able, by creating a hybrid with the contents of the conscious mind, to make sense of this energy and color, applying it as intended to solve intractable problems. In so doing, the ego is fortified qualitatively by benefitting from the animation process itself. It therefore is both an actor and acted upon, when the symbols do their magic. Animation is an activity without which the RGT metaphor is unable to fully bring about the outcomes you desire.

Animation (suspended): when you hit an obstacle during the animation process, because you stumble upon oppositional dilemmas or polarities that appear not to have a resolution.

Archetypes: they are unconscious content, which when it becomes conscious (through the symbol animation process) takes on the hue and reactions of the individual consciousness in which it appears. Archetypes can be seen as being to the psyche what instincts are to the body (Weinrib, 2004).

They are processes rather than things, and their action is felt by their impact (their change-work remains unconscious). The symbols simply are archetypal content clad in a form recognizable to the ego. Archetypal content as conveyed by symbols from the collective unconscious has a profound impact on our thoughts, thoughts about thoughts (self-reflection) and behavior.

Ego: this is the part of selfhood that we are consciously aware of and which we 'boot-up' every morning, subjectively identify as 'me' and are aware of (we are aware that we exist; or aware of being aware). The ego is therefore a subject (hence, subjective) and object at the same time. Ego is the smaller sliver of selfhood, even though its bravado can convince us that this is the whole 'me'. It must be emphasized that ego is necessary for the normal functioning of the personality. It is the part that makes contact with reality and has to flexibly integrate unconscious urges (in the Freudian sense) into the personality and the context of environmental pressures, including norms, values and other borrowed standards. However, the ego can often labor under delusions of grandeur (in the non-clinical sense). Its propensity to trade in the 'currency' of quantity rather than quality and its dependence on feedback from the environment often precludes it from fully experiencing the ecstasy of the abstract and more metaphysical dimensions that the 'Self' holds in store.

Emotional entropy: this is when emotions are no longer available/harnessed for purpose of change through animation. They become random, disorderly and even counter-productive. Oppositional dilemmas can fuel emotions to the extent that entropy results. Therefore, the resolution of the polarizations in the psyche have to be resolved to properly and constructively channel your emotions to achieve your outcome as per the RGT metaphor.

Meta: this means above and beyond. Metaphor is such as it provides insight into the structure and contents of one's thoughts; specifically the beneficiary domain. Metaphor has more 'intelligence' (thoughts about thoughts), thus enabling insight not only into our conscious minds but what our unconscious perceives to be a current and future state of our mental and life affairs (possibility).

Metaphor: the nature of metaphor is hinted at by the word element 'meta-' (meaning above and beyond). Metaphors are 'higher up' in our mental landscape than ordinary thoughts. They direct the manner in which we receive and attend to 'reality' (notably our inner reality) through our senses and thoughts. Metaphors contain a donor domain and a beneficiary domain. If we say, 'She has a heart of stone', the former is the beneficiary domain ('she') and the latter ('heart of stone') is the donor domain. The donor domain enriches the beneficiary domain by reflecting or signifying something about 'her' that enlightens us (and others). The same would apply to a RGT metaphor that is stated positively, e.g. 'She is like the wind.' This immediately is positive and facilitates the process of change as driven by the metaphor animation process.

Metaphor beneficiary: this is you, when the scenario (your wishes and desires) set out in the RGT metaphor comes to fruition.

Metaphor decoding: metaphor decoding is the result of the metaphor animation process. The latter imbues the symbols with energy, giving rise to new associations. A sudden burst of insight can result from altering (through animation) the meaning of the metaphor/insight into it as a whole and bring about personal transformation. Remedial or generative change often results from animating parts, but with the whole staying much like it is.

Metaphor envelope: by creating a RGT metaphor envelope, the unconscious 'creates' a field and makes it fruitful by placing initial symbols, which are mirrors or imitations of its desires as reflected in the metaphor in it. The envelope is the nexus between your conscious and unconscious mind. Jung speaks of a 'temenos – a piece of land, often a grove, set apart and dedicated to a god' (1974, p.127).

Metaphor precursors: these are steps on the way to the actual metaphor. For example, if you were to say, 'I am all wound up', this is the metaphor *pre-cursor*. This doesn't provide enough to work with. You would have to ask yourself, 'Wound up *LIKE WHAT*?' This will yield the negatively phrased metaphor which you can then convert into the RGT metaphor and subsequently animate, by looking at 'wound up like *how*?'

Metaphor types:
- Remedial
- Generative
- Transformative

Representation: 'reality' as experienced again (*re*-presentation) through our nervous system, based on memories and future expectations.

Self: this is the hypothetical summation of an indescribable whole – one half of it consists of ego-consciousness, the other of the shadow. The Self includes the collective unconscious and the archetypes. Symbols arise from here and are not the 'product' of the conscious ego, even though the latter contributes to it, as it does through the symbol animation process.

Shadow emotions: they refer to those emotions which 'pop up' almost immediately, 'behind' an initial emotion. They influence our subjective emotional state and how we think about things and act on them, by changing the first emotion. (Note: shadow emotions have nothing to do with the shadow as conceptualized by Carl Jung. By 'shadow', Jung meant the inferior aspects of personality which are denied manifestation in daily life (disowned), given their incompatibility with one's conscious attitude (or induce shame or guilt as they are perceived to clash with what is deemed as socially desirable). They are therefore shunted outside conscious awareness and form a converse manifestation in the unconscious.

Sub-sensory: this means 'underneath' our sensory experiences; that which makes up our experiences – their qualities and finer grain. An example is: 'That is a tall order.' The sub-sensory quality of the 'order' is that it is 'tall'. This is an important start or introduction to the animation process.

Symbols: they are change agents deployed by the unconscious mind. Their hallmark is that they are able to reconcile ostensibly irreconcilable opposites that the ego (the part of 'us' we are consciously aware of at any given time) is unable to deal with. At a most basic level, symbols bring forth new and sometimes groundbreaking insights.

Symbol color: the colors of your symbols are very important markers for your change process. As a formative principle of your instinctual power, the archetype's blue (color of air and sky: spiritual) is contaminated with red (warm color denoting emotions), making it appear violet (Jung). See whether, as you progress with the animation process, your symbols change in color, and how.

Symbol precursors: these are the contents of RGT metaphor prior to the animation process starting. They create the receptacles to 'receive' the actual symbols and to make them proliferate and reveal their meaning. You could think about this as creating a little garden with rich and fertile soil which is wet and poised to receive seeds.

Symbols (resource): different symbols have different remedial, generative or transformative propensities. Resource symbols appear specifically to achieve these outcomes. Their exact role and purpose becomes evident as the animation process comes to fruition and symbols start to 'interact' with each other in the metaphor envelope.

Symbol Sketch Pad (SSP): From the perspective of a workspace, the metaphor envelope is a SSP where you engage with and explore the symbols through the animation process.

References

Bateson, G. (1972). *Steps to an Ecology of Mind*. The University of Chicago Press.

Bradshaw (1988). *On the Family*. Florida: Health Communications.

Capra, F. (1997). *The Web of Life*. New York: Random House.

Carter, R. (2002). *Consciousness*. UK: Weidenfeld and Nicolson.

Edelman, G.M. (2004). *Wider than the Sky*. London: Penguin.

Edelman, G.M. & Tononi, G. (2000). *Consciousness. How matter becomes imagination*. London: Penguin.

Feldman, J.A. (2006). *From Molecule to Metaphor: A Neural Theory of Language*. Massachusetts: MIT.

Gregory, R. (1999).'Flagging the present with Qualia.' In Rose, S. (Ed). *From Brains to Consciousness: Essays on the New Sciences of the Mind*. Penguin.

Herr, C. (Undated). *Sheridan and the Field*. Film Institute of Ireland.

Johnson, M. and Lakoff, G. (2003). *Metaphors We Live By*. Chicago: University of Chicago Press.

Jung, C.G. (1995). *Memories, Dreams, Reflections*. Fontana Press.

Jung, C.G. (1989). *Aspects of the Masculine*. Routledge.

Jung, C.G. (1974). *Dreams*. Routledge.

Jung, C.G. (1972). *Four Archetypes*. Routledge.

Jung, C.G. (1969). *On the Nature of the Psyche*. Routledge.

Jung, C.G. (1959). *The Archetypes and the Collective Unconscious*. Princeton University Press.

Lawley, J. & Tompkins, P. (2000). *Metaphors in Mind*. The Developing Co. Press.

Lipton, B.H. (2005). *The Biology of Belief*. Santa Rosa: Mountain of Love/Elite Books.

Miller, G.A. (1956). 'The magical number seven, plus or minus two: Some limits on our capacity for processing information.' *The Psychological Review, 63*, 81–97.

Schwartz, J., Stapp, H.P and Beauregard, M. (2005). 'Quantum physics in neuroscience and psychology: A neurophysical model of mind-brain interaction.' *Philosophical Transactions of the Royal Society, 360*, 1309–1327.

Schwartz, J., (2002). *The Mind and the Brain: Neuroplasticity and the Power of Mental Force.* HarperCollins.

Senge, P. (1990). *The Fifth Discipline.* Random House.

Tacey, D. (2006). *How to Read Jung.* Granta Publications.

Turner, B.A. (2005). The *Handbook of Sandplay Therapy.* Temenos.

Weinrib, E. (2004). *The Sandplay Therapy Process: Images of the Self.* Temenos.

Wilson, C. (1984). *C.G. Jung: Lord of the Underworld.* The Aquarian Press.

B O O K S

mySpiritRadio